"I believe faith that gets out of the pew and goes out and just loves on hurting and broken people right where they are is the most powerful form of the gospel known to man. It is the exact ministry of Jesus. *How to Pick Up a Stripper and Other Acts of Kindness* illustrates beautifully this idea in action. This book could change your life and the way you live out what you believe!"

> Jeff Foxworthy
> Comedian and Host of *The American Bible Challenge*

"Service, generosity, kindness, outreach, compassion and love are just a few things you will pick up on when reading *How to Pick Up a Stripper and Other Acts of Kindness*. This book is not a how-to guide to start a stripper outreach—it is a how-to guide on how to live your life every day and see where God might lead you. You will walk away from reading this book with practical and tangible ideas for outreach and service in your local community, and maybe even your local strip club."

> Craig Gross
> Founder of XXXChurch.com and Strip Church

"Erin Stevens' passion for reaching women in the sex industry is contagious, and this book is even more contagious! It will leave you feeling inspired and ready to make an impact in your community the minute you start reading. In *How to Pick Up a Stripper and Other Acts of Kindness*, Todd and Erin share practical and spiritual tips on how anyone, whether young or old, introvert or extrovert, rich or poor, can change someone's life in their community by one practical act of kindness or generosity. I believe the heart and passion behind this book coincides with the compelling heart of Jesus."

> Tara Ulrich
> National Strip Church Coordinator

HOW TO
PICK UP A
STRIPPER

AND OTHER ACTS OF KINDNESS

TODD AND ERIN STEVENS

THOMAS NELSON
Since 1798

NASHVILLE   DALLAS   MEXICO CITY   RIO DE JANEIRO

Published in Nashville, Tennessee, by Thomas Nelson. Thomas Nelson is a trademark of HarperCollins Christian Publishing, Inc.

Thomas Nelson, Inc., titles may be purchased in bulk for educational, business, fund-raising, or sales promotional use. For information, please e-mail SpecialMarkets@ ThomasNelson.com.

Page design and layout: Crosslin Creative
Images: CanStockPhoto, BigStock

Unless otherwise indicated, Scripture quotations are taken from The Voice™ translation. © 2012 Ecclesia Bible Society. Used by permission. All rights reserved.*

Scripture quotations marked NASB are taken from the NEW AMERICAN STANDARD BIBLE®, © The Lockman Foundation 1960, 1962, 1963, 1968, 1971, 1972, 1973, 1975, 1977, 1995. Used by permission.

Scripture quotations marked NIV are taken from the Holy Bible, New International Version®, NIV®. Copyright © 1973, 1978, 1984, 2011 by Biblica, Inc.™ Used by permission of Zondervan. All rights reserved worldwide. www.zondervan.com

ISBN: 978-0-5291-1687-1

* Note: Italics in quotations from The Voice are used to "indicate words not directly tied to the dynamic translation of the original language" but that "bring out the nuance of the original, assist in completing ideas, and . . . provide readers with information that would have been obvious to the original audience" (The Voice, preface). Author emphasis in quotations from The Voice is indicated with the use of **boldface** type.

Printed in the United States of America

14 15 16 17 18 19 RRD 6 5 4 3 2 1

DEDICATION

Dedicated to Friendship Community Church,
aka "The Island of Misfit Toys"

ACKNOWLEDGMENTS

Special thanks . . .

To Katie and your two precious girls. May blessings and favor pour out on you for allowing us to share part of your incredible story.

To "the girls." Please don't ever forget that you are valuable to God and valuable to us.

To Neil and Mindi, who love us unconditionally and provide the friendship that every pastor's family needs.

To Elijah, Daniel, and Levi, who are mighty men of God in their generation. You are game changers for the kingdom of God, and we cannot wait to see what God has in store for your surrendered lives. We love you all the way.

To our parents, who believed in the vision of Friendship Community Church from the beginning.

To John. Thank you for not saying no.

To Jason and Julie, who have been our cheerleaders and sounding board.

To Teri, the best career placement person in town. Thank you for being a vital part of Nashville Strip Church.

To Kathy, who filled our freezer with delicious food. Our family is blessed by your generosity and kindness.

To Maleah, our editor and friend, who saw the potential for this book.

To Jesus, who showed us how to love and serve people. We worship You and give You all the praise that is in us.

CONTENTS

FOREWORD

Sometimes when we "talk" to others outside our spiritual ring, our words come out sounding a lot like a foreign language. The problem isn't just that we only speak English. What's more we speak with a particular accent, depending on where we live. Imagine for a moment that most people don't understand what we are saying.

Let's learn how to speak the way those around can understand, whatever that may be. Todd and Erin Stevens have started a church that focuses on the international language of "Kindness that changes everything." The story of what has happened in Nashville shows there are lots of people who speak the same mother tongue.

God made each of us with needs and desires that are impossible to ignore. It's also true that all of us need to experience kindness and generosity. We are vulnerable to it, so when we experience it our hearts rejoice. We think, "So this is the way life is supposed to work."

As you read this book, imagine yourself as a dry sponge that needs a good soaking. Put aside your expectations of what outreach or evangelism is "supposed" to look like. Let the waters of newness soak their way in and allow for a new perspective. I believe you will look back in five years and agree that this will have been one of the most influential books you've read.

Steve Sjogren
Author & Coach, Kindness.com

GETTING STARTED

We had no idea about the journey God had in store for us.

I'm a pastor, and my wife hangs out in strip clubs. I used to be a computer programmer, and she was a human resources director. We were respectable and successful people and had lots of respectable and successful friends. Then God showed up and wrecked all of that. I'm so glad He did.

When my wife, Erin, and I first started meeting with the group of people who would become the launch team for Friendship Community Church in 2006, we had no idea about the journey God had in store for us. The group that assembled for those first planning meetings had a shared vision for a church that would actively demonstrate God's love in our community in practical ways by meeting needs and doing acts of kindness. We believed God could use this type of church to change the face of our city.

Since that time, we've been blessed to see transformation begin in our community. We've had the opportunity to see hundreds of lives radically changed by the message of Jesus. But the change that has occurred in Erin and me has been even more radical.

Erin used to hang out primarily with other suburban moms, and the only dancers she knew were the ones on *Dancing with the Stars*. Now she leads a ministry called Nashville Strip Church, which is reaching out to the dancers and other employees of inner-city strip clubs with the message of God's love.

I used to spend all my time with people who had been in church for most of their lives. The closest I had been to any kind of addiction was my own infatuation with pepperoni pizza. Now my circle of friends includes addicts and ex-cons. When we first began the church, I'm not sure I even knew those people existed in my community. Now I can't imagine what my life would be like without them.

The purpose of this book is to share with you what we've learned along the way, so you can make an even greater impact for God in your community. I'll bet that reaching your community will even be easier and more fun than you think. I have no doubt God can use you to make a difference and

> Now my circle of friends includes addicts and ex-cons.

advance His kingdom. If He can use me, then that proves He really can use anybody.

I (Todd) am doing the writing, and Erin will be looking over my shoulder and telling me whenever I get something wrong. I'll make whatever changes she suggests; then I'll change it back to the way I like it when she leaves the room. In case you were wondering, she's out of the room as I write this part, or else I would never have gotten away with that last sentence.

IT'S TIME FOR SHOW-AND-TELL

I always loved it in elementary school when we got to do "show-and-tell." This was my opportunity to show my friends the new batting glove I got for Christmas or to bring a picture of my grandparents. Then I'd tell them all about whatever I had brought. Those days were always fun and interesting, even though none of the third graders in my class were public-speaking prodigies. Their speech, or "tell," didn't have to be great, because it was accompanied by the "show."

The highlight from that time for me was when my friend Jim busted out his awesome baseball card collection. In case you're too young to have ever been excited about baseball cards, just imagine old-school Pokémon cards, except with actual athletes instead of some evolution of a Pikachu. Anyway, Jim was a hardcore collector. For some baseball seasons, he had the cards for every player on every team.

Jim had lots of good information too. He could talk about Dave Winfield's stats and why George Brett's rookie card was already worth so much. As he gave his speech, I could hold his cards in my hand and see them up close. I could see immediately that my cards, with their bent corners and frayed edges, were way inferior to his. I had a front-row seat to what could happen when a regular guy like Jim took better care of his cards. The combination of show-and-tell inspired me to make some changes. I knew I could do it because I now had the right information and a good example.

I've never been a bold, outspoken person who could just walk up to anyone and begin a conversation. As I grew in my Christian faith, I started looking for ways to share it with others. I wanted to do exactly what Jesus had commanded: "Therefore go and make disciples of all nations, baptizing them in the name of the Father and of the Son and of the Holy Spirit, and teaching them to obey everything I have commanded you" (Matt. 28:19–20 NIV).

Unfortunately, whenever I tried to "go and make disciples," I usually ended up feeling like a failure. I went to training classes and read books because I really wanted to help other people connect with God. I had no doubt that every person's life (and eternity) would be exponentially better if Jesus were in the center of it.

But whenever I would try to do evangelism, instead of making disciples, I was just making people uncomfortable. It felt as if I were putting on a shoe that just didn't fit right. Actually, a better comparison to my attempts at evangelism would be that it was like me as a two-hundred-pound-guy putting on pink high heels. Not only was it painful for me, but it was painful to watch. I was focused exclusively on the "tell."

When I first read Steve Sjogren's groundbreaking book *Conspiracy of Kindness*, I had finally found the shoe that fit. I'm wanting to make an analogy to being like Cinderella finding her glass slipper, but then that would be another analogy that has me wearing women's shoes, so let's not go there.

In his book, Steve unpacked the concept of *servant evangelism*. Servant evangelism is an approach to outreach that isn't just about telling people the gospel: it is about showing them too. I was intrigued. Could it really be possible to do evangelism without coming across as obnoxious or manipulative, as I had in the past? It occurred to me for the first time that this was what Jesus had done.

In his account of the life of Jesus, Matthew wrote, "Jesus went throughout Galilee. He taught in the synagogues. He preached the good news of the Kingdom, and He healed people, ridding their bodies of sickness and disease" (Matt. 4:23). He taught and preached the good news *and* he met people's physical needs.

Could it really be possible to do evangelism without coming across as obnoxious or manipulative?

If Jesus had only taught lessons and not done the good works, I think the crowds would have been smaller, and would have consisted mostly of intellectuals and religious people. If He had gone around healing everybody, but never taught them the truth about God, then crowds of people would have shown up to be entertained, but they would have never changed or grown spiritually. Jesus always did both.

Servant evangelism is about doing both—showing and telling. Words without good deeds lack credibility. Good deeds without words lack eternal impact.[1] As followers of Jesus, we're challenged to do both.

As we serve people and do acts of kindness, their hearts open up and they often want to know more about why we're doing what we're doing. Whether we have an in-depth conversation or just hand them a card explaining that we're showing God's love in a practical way, they leave the encounter with a more positive view of Christianity and a tangible experience of God's love. Servant evangelism is about both *serving* and *evangelizing*, so we'll define what we mean by both of those words in the pages ahead.

Servant evangelism is about doing both— showing and telling.

For now, maybe an example will help. I eat lunch at Subway almost every day. I figure if Jared lost 250 pounds eating those sandwiches, then I can't possibly go wrong. A while back I decided to start paying every day for the person's lunch who was in line behind me. The employees have caught on and know I'm going to do it now. They get excited every time.

As I pick up the tab, I hand the person behind me a business-sized card and say, "Lunch is on me today. I just wanted to do this to show you God's love in a practical way with no strings attached." The card (which I ordered from ServantEvangelism .com) has basically the same thing as what I said on one side, and the other side has some basic information about our church.

Each day as I am driving to Subway, I pray that God will put just the right person in line behind me. Today when I went to lunch, my recipient was an elderly woman. At first, she didn't understand what I was doing. Then we had a nice conversation as we got our drinks. She told me a bit about the church she attends and thanked me for what I had done.

This evening I received an e-mail from a young lady who attends our church. She told me that her neighbor from two doors down, Dot, had come to see her this evening. Dot knew this young lady attended Friendship and wanted to tell her about the handsome young man who had bought her lunch today. Okay, I added in the "handsome" part.

Anyway, it turns out that Dot is caring for her forty-nine-year-old son who has Down syndrome and lives with her. Her husband died many years ago, and her daughter has just recently filed for disability. Even though Dot's only income is her Social Security check, she is now buying the groceries for all three of them. Do you think God put just the right person in line behind me to receive a free lunch as an expression of His love? I am continually amazed at the ways God uses my daily lunch gift.

That may sound to you like a nice thing to do for someone, but it may not seem to be evangelism. After all, nobody "prayed the prayer," and I didn't even mention what Jesus did on the cross. That is okay if it doesn't all make sense yet. By the end of this book, you'll understand just how potent a simple act of kindness can be in reaching people with the gospel.

There are lots of good ways to do evangelism. I think most of us want to be able to reach people and share our faith. If you are already effective in communicating the gospel to people so that they often understand and respond, then by all means please keep doing what you're doing.

If you're like I was, though, and are looking for a practical way to connect with people in the real world and to see them take the next step toward God from wherever they are, then perhaps servant evangelism will be the shoe that fits you just right. I think you're going to enjoy learning these concepts and seeing what God does as you put them into practice.

WE DON'T NEED A BUILDING, BUT OUR COMMUNITY DOES

Since its inception, Friendship has engaged in servant evangelism by showing God's love in practical ways with no strings attached.[2] I kept a separate full-time job for the first year, so the church could devote more of its resources to meeting needs and reaching out in our community. I had an office in our basement and was the only staff at the time, so we didn't see a need for any additional space for our church besides the school we rented each Sunday for our worship services.

As the church began to grow, the size of our student group grew too. We kept shifting our growing youth group to bigger and bigger houses, until we finally decided they needed a space of their own for their midweek gathering. So we rented some space in a storefront that had a couple of large meeting rooms and some small offices on the side. We dubbed it the CITY—Christ Is Transforming Youth.

We'd only had the space at the CITY for a few months when Middle Tennessee was hit by its biggest disaster since the Civil War. You may not have heard much about it because some national news outlets devoted only fifteen minutes of total coverage to the event. The oil spill in the Gulf of Mexico was already dominating headlines, and there was a failed car bomb attempt in Times Square on the day the rain started. But for the people who were impacted, the flood that devastated Nashville in 2010 will never be forgotten. The total cost of the damage was in the billions of dollars. By some estimates, it was the costliest non-hurricane natural disaster in U.S. history.

In retrospect, the strangest part is that in this era of high-definition Doppler radar and ten-day forecasts, nobody saw this coming. When the rain began to fall on Saturday, it was just another storm. By Sunday morning, there were a few roads covered with water, but I was still able to make it to the school to begin setting up for our weekend worship experience. Within an hour, we realized we had a crisis on our hands because every road leading to the school had completely flooded. We would be trapped if we didn't get out fast. So we canceled the service, told everyone to stay home, and posted the sermon as a podcast on our website.

Thirteen inches of rain fell in just thirty-six hours, and the rainfall ultimately exceeded seventeen inches. Just imagine if a foot and a half of water were dumped over your entire region all at the same time. There just wasn't any place for all that water to go. Houses and buildings were literally washed away, and several lives were lost. But the flood had a very peculiar effect on the people of Nashville.

Within hours, it seemed as if everyone I knew had updated their Facebook profiles with this mantra: we are Nashville. Instead of the chaos and crime that other areas had experienced in the wake of disaster, the community rallied and people did whatever needed to be done to help their neighbors. Best of all, churches were leading the way in the relief effort, and Friendship was no exception. Our church was literally the first on the scene in two flooded communities. We rescued people with boats and ATVs. We brought food and bottled water. Along with the supplies, we gave flood victims a simple card with our phone number and a message saying that we had volunteers standing by who were ready to meet whatever need they had.

Many of our people took days or weeks of vacation time from their jobs so they could serve the people around them.

Many of our people took days or weeks of vacation time from their jobs so they could serve the people around them. At the CITY, we set up a whiteboard that we used to log calls as they came in. Teams of volunteers arrived at our facility throughout the day to get an assignment from the board. Then they would head out to meet the need. Whether people needed someone to help them clean and dry their homes with a wet/dry shop vacuum, a team to come and tear out ruined drywall and flooring, or people with a truck to haul off ruined furniture and perhaps bring replacement furniture in, we did everything we could.

We are still so grateful for the churches from around the country that routed supplies to us as we provided aid for the flood victims. For a few weeks, the CITY looked more like a stockpile warehouse than a student center. The space was so full of inventory that at times it was hard to even walk between the aisles. Our relief efforts culminated with a completely free "yard sale" for flood victims, where we gave away everything we had received to our neighbors in need.

GO FEED THE STRIPPERS

After we got past the immediate aftermath of the flood, we assessed our response as a church and talked about what lessons we had learned. That was when we became aware for the first time just how valuable our leased space, which a few months earlier didn't even exist, had been in allowing us to serve our community. It began to dawn on us that even though we had always focused on meeting whatever needs we could, there were other needs our church either wouldn't be able to meet adequately or could not meet at all until we began taking steps toward a permanent ministry space dedicated to that purpose. This realization led to our dream for the Impact Center.

We began to envision a ministry mall where physical, relational, emotional, and spiritual needs could be met, all under one roof. This type of facility would allow us to increase our capacity to both meet needs and reach people with the message of Jesus. We could launch brand-new ministries that we had previously only dreamed about, like a respite ministry, which provides a parent's night out for families of kids with special needs. We would be able to expand existing ministries, like our food pantry for hungry people, our addiction recovery programs, and our job skills training.

Space could be allocated for other nonprofits with whom we already partnered so that together we could provide a counseling center, basic health care services for the uninsured, assistance for those with crisis pregnancies, and citizenship and language training for immigrants and refugees. The building itself would even be a disaster relief shelter, where we had our own volunteers trained and certified, so we could have a fully operational relief shelter within minutes of a disaster in our area.

In our community, when people are in need of electronics, they know they can go to Best Buy to grab a laptop or DVD player. If people here want sporting goods, they have two options: Academy Sports and Dick's Sporting Goods. When they have a craving for Mexican food, they probably just need to look left and right because we have more options for chips and queso dip than I can count. They are probably within a hundred yards of one at any given moment. But where do they go when they feel as though there's no hope?[3] Where can they turn when there's a crisis in their lives?

When a person in our community was in need of hope or help, we wanted their first

As you become the person God intends for you to become, you will reach the people God intends for you to reach.

thought to be, *I'll bet the Impact Center has something for me.* If people needed help with their marriage, there would be classes and counseling available. If they weren't sure how to put food on the table for their family, they would know they could come to get groceries. Whether they were trying to figure out how to be a better parent or their finances were a mess or they were struggling with an addiction, the Impact Center would be a place where they could find whatever help they needed.

We believed that God wanted a place like the Impact Center to exist in our community, where people could come with needs and be touched by someone who would show them God's love. *Outreach* magazine recently listed the Impact Center as one of the twenty-five most innovative ideas they had found for engaging the culture and reaching the community. But to us, it was just the logical next step.[4] So we began taking steps toward making this dream a reality as a gift to our community.

In the fall of 2012, Erin embarked on a twenty-one-day fast. This wasn't an extreme weight-loss scheme. She was desperate to see the Impact Center come to fruition, so she devoted herself to spending more time in prayer for our community and our church as she prayed toward that end. As her time of fasting neared completion, her focus began to shift from what could happen someday in the future when we had the building of our dreams to what could happen today in a completely different building.

Erin told me she felt that she needed to begin reaching out to strippers. When she first told me, I wasn't sure whether I should pretend not to know what a strip club was or what. Since we had already seen how powerful servant evangelism could be in so many different settings, we decided she should start by finding a way to show strippers God's love by serving them. So she called the manager of the biggest strip club in Nashville and asked whether she could bring a free, fully catered meal for everyone who worked there. The manager had only one question: "Could you come next Thursday?"

I'm sure some churches would frown on this sort of outreach or want answers to lots of questions before they started something so unconventional. But because of the type of ministry Friendship had already been doing and the type of people we had always focused on reaching, for us it just made sense. When I first mentioned it to our people in a sermon, they applauded. They immediately wanted to know what they could do to help. We even had several guys volunteer to help out, but taking guys to do ministry in a strip club seemed like a worse idea than asking Fran Drescher to sing the national anthem at the Super Bowl.

So Erin put together a team of ladies, and Nashville Strip Church was born. The results have been incredible. Now whenever I see a strip club, I see the potential for God to do something amazing.

PLEASE REMAIN SEATED; THE RIDE IS ABOUT TO BEGIN

In this book, we've included a lot of specific examples and shared the lessons we've learned as we've implemented these principles within our cultural context of a suburban community in the southern part of the United States. We'll return often to the story of what God has done through Strip Church because it wonderfully illustrates so much of what servant evangelism (which I interchangeably call "kindness outreach") is about. We'll share some other stories too. But I don't want to simply give you a bunch of tips and projects to try out, which may or may not be useful in your specific situation. I want you to understand *why* kindness outreach is such an effective approach to outreach. Once you know the basis, you'll be able to think of creative ways to apply this concept in a way that is relevant to any setting.

Understanding the underlying principles is absolutely crucial, because here is the biggest lesson we've learned: *as you become the person God intends for you to become, you will reach the people God intends for you to reach.* This book is about helping you become that person. By no means am I suggesting you have to focus on becoming better and better until you're finally worthy of reaching other people. Effectiveness in outreach isn't as much about how far along you are in your journey as it is what direction you're moving.

> **Effectiveness in outreach isn't as much about how far along you are in your journey as it is what direction you're moving.**

I have no doubt you want your life to count for something significant. I know you want to reach your full potential and to help other people begin their own relationships with God. The principles in this book will help you cultivate a heart and a lifestyle that reflect God's love in such an attractive way it is almost irresistible.

If you want to help other people connect with God and His amazing love, then it's absolutely vital you start with the right motivation, because if your motivation is simply to make a difference in your community through service projects (as admirable as that may be), you'll give up when you stop seeing tangible results and the going gets tough. If your motivation is to grow your church (which is not a bad goal either), then you'll get frustrated when attendance decreases or people stay home because it rained. But when you are motivated by a heart that beats for people the way God's heart does, then you will be unstoppable as you begin impacting your community for Christ, because God's heart for people will never change, and there will always be people who need to experience His love.

The key is that you get started. This book isn't about theory and academia. It is about getting started with allowing God to use you in your community to show who He is. So we have included specific actions steps for you to take, along with questions you can consider on your own or discuss in a group setting to determine how you are going to live out what you are learning. If a pastor's wife can use these principles to reach a stripper, with whom she would seem to have nothing in common, then perhaps you can use them even more effectively to reach people with whom you have tons in common. If that ex-stripper can then learn to use these same principles to help other strippers connect with God's love, then perhaps you can use them to reach your own coworkers. So let's get started—this really is going to be fun.

> **When you are motivated by a heart that beats for people the way God's heart does, then you will be unstoppable as you begin impacting your community for Christ.**

DISCUSSION QUESTIONS

- Spiritual growth is a process. As you think back on the process you've gone through to grow spiritually, what is a way your perspective has changed?

- When it comes to evangelism, what is your biggest fear?

- Matthew 4:23 tells how crowds came to Jesus because of the way He was serving them, and then they heard him preach. Why do you think selfless compassion has the power to turn heads and cause people to notice?

- Servant evangelism is simply showing God's love in a practical way with no strings attached. Whether with a group or by yourself, have you ever done anything like this? What happened?

- To reach the people God intends for us to reach, we need to become the people God intends for us to be. What is one area of your life you know needs to change for you to become more like the person God intends for you to be?

BUILD THE RIGHT REPUTATION

If someone summarized you with one word, what do you think he or she would say?

At least once a month, somebody here in the Nashville area tells me I look like Vince Gill. I'm fairly certain Vince is told just as often that he looks like me. Maybe not, but I like to think he hears it all the time. Once when someone was convinced I was Vince, I played along and signed an autograph. It was on the back of an IHOP receipt. I seriously hope she never tried to sell that scrap of paper on eBay. But if you did ever pay someone for an autographed IHOP receipt, please don't expect a refund from me.

Vince has a well-earned reputation as a singer and a fairly generous guy. He performs often at benefit concerts and is involved in lots of charity work. So when people think I am Vince, they automatically make assumptions about *me* because of what they have heard about *him*. I can usually keep the charade alive until somebody asks me to either sing one of Vince's hits or to kick-start his or her fund-raiser. At that point, the jig is up. I'm really not disappointed when people finally realize I am not him. The truth is I have no desire to be him. While I am sure Vince has a pretty good life, I'm actually trying to establish quite a different reputation—one that I think even he would want.

ONE-WORD REPUTATION

Everybody has a reputation. A good reputation can open doors of opportunity, while a bad one can be a difficult barrier to overcome. Some of the most well-known people and organizations even have reputations that can be summed up with a single word. For example, when I think about Billy Graham, the word that immediately comes to mind is *integrity*. Toyota? *Quality.* Southwest Airlines? *Inexpensive.* Miley Cyrus? *Twerking.* Donald Trump? *Wealth.* And *hair.* And *"You're fired."* Okay, that was a bad example.

If someone summarized you with one word, what do you think he or she would say? I dare you to ask somebody and find out. You may be surprised at what your reputation with other people actually is. I double-dog dare you to ask somebody in your community what your church is known for. Based on the conversations I've had with people in different communities, it seems as though most churches are known for their Bible classes and for giving Christians a place to hang out. Most churches seem to be pleased with that identity. It is crazy to think I was a Christian for forty years before I realized Jesus had articulated precisely what reputation I should be aiming for.

The night before Jesus was arrested, He gave His closest followers some final instructions: "I give you a new command: Love each other *deeply and fully*. Remember the ways that I have loved you, and demonstrate your love for others in those same ways. **Everyone will know you as My followers if you demonstrate your love to others**" (John 13:34–35, bold emphasis added).

Jesus could not have been more clear. He wanted people to be able to recognize His followers based on one thing and one thing only. It wasn't how much scripture they knew. It wasn't how well they recited a memorized gospel presentation. It wasn't even how much they looked like an undeniably handsome country music legend. He boiled it down to one word that He wanted to define their reputation: love. It was all about how they demonstrated love to one another and to the people in their community.

The twelve guys who heard Jesus speak these words had just spent three amazing years with Him. They had seen Him do miracles that were hard to describe and heard Him teach lessons that were revolutionary. Even as the crowds had swelled and it seemed as if everyone was clamoring for His time, His disciples were the ones who knew Him best. Jesus knew each of them intimately too. As they

> Jesus boiled it down to one word that He wanted to define His disciples' reputation: love.

traveled together, He saw them at their best and their worst. So when Jesus told them to remember the ways He had loved them, they each had very specific and personal memories about how He had done just that.

Matthew must have thought back to the day when Jesus had walked up to his tax collector's booth. Most Jews would have considered Matthew a traitor, a sell-out, and a social reject because of the way he extorted taxes from his own people. But Jesus had simply said, "Follow Me" (Matt. 9:9), and then gone to his house for lunch with him and his tax collector buddies. Even though associating with an outcast like Matthew could potentially diminish His prestige and tarnish His image, Jesus demonstrated nothing but love.[1]

Nathanael, who is presumed to be the same man as the apostle Bartholomew, probably thought back to how, when he had first heard Philip suggest that Jesus might be the long-awaited Messiah, he had sarcastically responded, "How can anything good come from *a place like* Nazareth?" (John 1:46). In that day, Nazareth was basically known as the home to rednecks and hillbillies. To Nathanael, Philip's remark was like hearing someone say the Christ was Honey Boo Boo's first cousin. It just didn't compute. But even though Jesus knew how Nathanael had dissed him, He demonstrated nothing but love.

Perhaps Peter thought back to the fateful day when he and the other disciples were out in a boat and got caught in gale-force winds and crashing waves. Without Dramamine or a life preserver, he had stepped out in faith and for a few spectacular seconds walked on water. Then he looked at the storm and remembered, *Wait a minute—I'm Peter.* That was when he sank like a rock. After this disappointing performance, I almost expect Jesus to say, "Sorry, Peter. You just don't have what it takes to be a disciple. Thanks for playing. We have some lovely parting gifts for you." Instead, He demonstrated nothing but love.

WHEN YOU AIM YOUR LOVE AT OTHERS, YOU CAN'T MISS

Each of those original followers knew exactly how they were supposed to love other people because they remembered exactly how Jesus had loved them. What about you? Perhaps you have been more of an outcast than Matthew, had more issues to overcome than Nathanael, and feel you've disappointed God more than Peter. Jesus has never stopped loving you. He gave His life for you. Nothing you have ever done or ever will do could cause Him to love you any less. He wants you to remember how He has loved you, and then start demonstrating that same kind of love to other people.

Since Jesus founded the church, it only makes sense that He would define the desired reputation: be known for love. Jesus brilliantly loved people into life change. He also made it clear that His followers aren't just supposed to love the other insiders. Our love is supposed to have an outward focus too.

Once, as Jesus was responding to a question from a group of Sadducees, a scribe overheard Him and recognized the wisdom in His answer. A scribe's job was to study the Hebrew Scriptures and meticulously copy them by hand, so that the law and the writings of the prophets could be preserved and passed on to future generations. He was the first-century equivalent of a document scanner with optical character recognition. His entire life revolved around God's law, and at some point a question about it had developed in his mind. Perhaps this was his chance to find out the answer.

> **Scribe:** Tell me, Teacher. What is the most important thing that God commands *in the law*?
>
> **Jesus:** The most important commandment is this: "Hear, O Israel, the Eternal One is our God, and the Eternal One is the only God. You should love the Eternal, your God, with all your heart, with all your soul, with all your mind, and with all your strength." The second *great commandment* is this: "Love others in the same way you love yourself." There are no commandments more important than these. (Mark 12:28–31)

Jesus made it clear that what is most important is that we have a loving relationship with God and loving relationships with the people around us. If you have a relationship with God, then your life is going to be increasingly characterized by love. This kind of love will then impact the way you treat other people. In fact, you can measure the depth and maturity of your vertical love for God by the extent of your horizontal love for the people around you (1 John 3:17; 4:20–21).

That is why at Friendship Community Church we continually encourage our people to be sold out to do whatever it takes to be known as the most loving people in our area. We are absolutely convinced that the best way to reach people in our community and invite them to take the next step toward a relationship with God is to let them experience His love through us. Our small groups and care teams make sure we are effectively showing love and meeting the needs that exist within the church, but never at the expense of losing our outward focus.

When we aim our love outward, we can't miss. Everybody you meet can benefit from a tangible expression of care. Since our goal as Christians is to become more loving, and since everyone wants to be loved, it's hard to imagine a more natural way to reach others than demonstrating God's love.

> He wants you to remember how He has loved you, and then start demonstrating that same kind of love to other people.

Our goal is to love our community in such a way that if we closed the doors tomorrow and ceased to exist as a church, then even the people who had never visited us on a Sunday would miss us terribly. We know that will only happen if we demonstrate love for them at a level they have never before experienced and would have never expected. That is why we are constantly getting our people engaged with showing God's love in the community through efforts such as giving away a full tractor-trailer load of groceries, hosting a community-wide Easter Bash, providing free oil changes for single parents, playing bingo at senior centers, and tutoring refugees as they prepare for their citizenship exams.

We do everything we can to be known for how we demonstrate love to others. That is even why we always wear the same bright-orange shirts with our church logo when we're serving in the community. The shirts have become a distinctive that has helped us build a reputation. When people in our community see those easily recognizable shirts, they now immediately know they're seeing a group of people showing God's love through serving others. In fact, as we were explaining the shirts at a recent 101 church orientation class, one of our new attenders said, "I didn't realize that this was the orange-shirt church! This is the church I was looking for!"

If you want to build a reputation for love, be intentional about it. Put it on your calendar, and seize every opportunity that comes your way. In a self-centered culture, it really is not that hard to stand out from the crowd when you point your love outward and do things that are selfless and sacrificial.

FULL OF GRACE, SEASONED WITH SALT

As you read through the New Testament, one thing becomes abundantly clear: spiritual maturity is far more about how well you love than how much you know. It's ironic, then, that the outreach training in most churches assumes that the key to reaching people with the gospel is simply more information. I know this because I've made the same assumption and done the same thing.

Most evangelism training begins with memorizing a script and some key Bible verses, which may or may not always be used in the proper context. This was how I learned to do outreach and how I taught other people too. We would use acronyms to help us commit our gospel speech to memory, because our goal was to get this set of facts crammed into our heads until we could recite them word for word. I would have everyone rehearse their monologues to each other because our assumption was that if we could just explain the facts clearly enough, then people would respond and would begin meaningful relationships with God. Once we had our speeches perfected, we were ready to go knock on some doors and bless people with our scripted pitch.

But what if our premise about evangelism was entirely wrong?

Not long ago we had a vacuum cleaner salesman at our house. Erin had scheduled the appointment because she was convinced this machine was the one appliance that would bring so much domestic bliss that our home would look like a Norman Rockwell painting. I decided to sit in on the meeting because I hadn't noticed any major problems with our carpet in the past, so I wasn't sure we really needed a new vacuum. If my wallet was going to be involved, then I wanted to have some say in the final verdict.

Overall, the salesman's presentation was impressive. He was charming, had lots of facts and statistics, and was quick to answer our questions. At one point, he poured an entire cup of salt onto our carpet. He then insisted that I walk on the salt to grind it into the carpet a bit, so I hesitantly complied. He then cleaned the salty spot with our old vacuum cleaner. The carpet looked pretty good, or so I thought. He pulled out the demonstration filter and showed me that my trusty old vacuum had picked up only about a fourth of a cup of salt. This was not good. There was still three-quarters of a cup of salt embedded in my carpet.

He assured me this was not a problem because he had the solution. Then he allowed me to use his amazing device to experience for myself how easy it was to extract the rest of the salt from the carpet. For the grand finale, he revealed that his machine had sucked up another half cup of salt that my pitiful vacuum cleaner had left behind. I felt it was my duty to point out to him that based on my calculations (1/4 + 1/2 = not done yet), there was still a fourth of a cup of salt in the carpet that had not been accounted for. I asked if he had a plan for how to get the rest of the salt out. He assured me that I was mistaken because the carpet was now so clean it was practically sterilized.

About this time, our dog came in and started licking the spot in question. I made a comment about it being funny that the dog was so interested in licking a spot where there was (according to him) no salt. He didn't think it was as funny as I did.

A well-rehearsed speech is a great approach to selling vacuum cleaners, but it's a lousy way to spread the gospel.

Here's my point—at no time during his polished presentation did I ever have the thought *I think this guy really loves me*. Instead, I was very clear about his agenda. He wanted to make a sale and earn a commission. He wanted something *from* me. His goal was to establish just enough of a rapport with me to seal the deal. Then he was going to move on to the next customer. The odds were slim that he and I would be hanging out or going to watch a movie together, especially after the salt incident.

A well-rehearsed speech is a great approach to selling vacuum cleaners, but it's a lousy way to spread the gospel. When our starting point for outreach is anything but love for the person, we are off target and will miss the mark. There is ultimately nothing wrong with memorizing a gospel presentation. In fact, it can be a great way for us to build confidence in our ability to understand and communicate the basic facts. But when our starting point for sharing those facts isn't love, we reduce the gospel to a sales pitch. We have to begin by developing a heart that truly loves people and wants what is best for them. That will only happen as we spend time with God, receiving His love, and spend time with people, allowing His love to flow through us.

It may seem odd to begin a book on outreach discussing the type of reputation we need to have, but that is precisely the point. When it comes to outreach, love has to be the starting point, the ending point, and everything in between. For too long the church has tried to do outreach by only *telling* people about God's love, rather than *demonstrating* God's love. What is keeping most people from taking the next step toward Christ isn't that they simply need more information about the gospel: they need a demonstration of the gospel. Paul reminded the church at Corinth that even if we say and do all the right things, our graceful words and noble actions ultimately have no value if they aren't rooted in love.

What if I speak in the *most elegant* languages of people or in the *exotic* languages of the heavenly messengers, but I live without love? Well then, anything I say is like the clanging of brass or a crashing cymbal . . . I could give all that I have to feed the poor, I could surrender my body to be burned *as a martyr*, but if I do not live in love, I gain nothing *by my selfless acts*. (1 Cor. 13:1, 3)

I've met lots of church people who claimed to follow Jesus, but acted like total jerks. I'll bet you have known a few of those too. So have most of the people I've met who say they want nothing to do with God or the church. Many of the people I meet have attended church before, perhaps regularly at some point. They have heard the information about Jesus and may even believe some of it. What most walked away from was some form of inauthenticity. Maybe they were turned off by blatant hypocrisy, or maybe they simply got their feelings hurt. Either way, kindness can communicate genuineness and gives a person hope that perhaps a right relationship with God really is possible.

Here is the reality: it is hard for people to believe that Jesus cares about them when they are sure His followers don't. They are repelled when they see that sort of hypocrisy. They think they are rejecting Jesus, but all they have really seen in us is a caricature of Him. We need to show them the real deal. We need to be known for how we show God's love. Because when people encounter a genuine expression of God's love through an otherwise ordinary person, it is almost irresistible.

I HAVEN'T HEARD OF THAT GOD

I met a humble guy named Nicko on a recent mission trip to Quito, Ecuador. He is in his early twenties and has already established several amazing ministries there. One issue he is especially focused on is human trafficking. When he first decided to do something about it, he went and stood outside a well-known brothel and held up a poster. It read: "Real men don't have to buy their women." Seriously. He said he didn't connect with a lot of people that day, but he also didn't get beat up. I was impressed, not only by his boldness, but by the fact that he didn't get pulverized by the people who owned the brothel.

He went back the next week with a few ladies and a new approach. They brought flowers for the prostitutes working on the corner. They talked with them and listened to their stories. They asked how they could help make the girls' lives better. Some of the girls were there by choice, but most were there because their "owner" required it. Nicko and his team explained how God loved them and had always loved them. They told the girls that it is never too late for a second chance with Him.

The girls' response was revealing. They were drawn in by this demonstration of compassion. They said other people had come and told them about God before, but had only talked about judgment and condemnation. They asked Nicko, "What God is this you are talking about? Because we must have heard about a different God."

We need to be sure we present to people the Jesus who is known for how He loves. Jesus loves them no matter what they've done, just as He loves us no matter what we've done. We need to be very clear that *what* a person has done is not the same as *who* that person is. Those are two completely different things. Prostituting may be what someone once did. Stripping may be what someone did. Looking at porn may be what someone did. But what a person has done does not define who he or she is. Aren't you glad you don't have to live the rest of your life being defined by what you've done in the past? You are not defined by

Jesus loves people no matter what they've done, just as He loves us no matter what we've done.

your temper or your divorce or your abortion or your biggest regret. Jesus sees all of that stuff and still loves you and says you are completely forgivable.

People already have enough guilt and shame. What they need is someone like you who can demonstrate God's love for them. Sharing your faith isn't about selling Jesus the same way an infomercial might do. Jesus never treated people like targets. He wasn't a slick salesman who wanted something *from* people purely for His own benefit. He loved them and wanted something *for* them. We need to be the same way.

Genuine compassion is incredibly influential. If you think about it, you already know from firsthand experience about the influential power of unconditional love. Even though you and I have probably never met, here is what I know about you: the people who have had the biggest positive impact on your life have been those who loved you the most completely, with no strings attached. They may not have been the smartest people, they certainly weren't perfect, and some of them may not have even been Christians. But you knew without a doubt they loved you. Because they did, they have influenced your life in profound ways. That is the power of love.

FREQUENTLY ASKED QUESTION

As an old man, the apostle John reflected back on how Jesus had demonstrated love for others. He wrote, "This is how we know what love is: Jesus Christ laid down his life for us. And we ought to lay down our lives for our brothers and sisters. If anyone has material possessions and sees a brother or sister in need but has no pity on them, how can the love of God be in that person? Dear children, let us not love with words or speech but with actions and in truth" (1 John 3:16–18 NIV).

My wife, Erin, is an absolute prayer warrior. After an extended time of praying and fasting, God laid a new burden on her heart: to begin showing His love to employees of strip clubs. When the manager of the largest strip club in Nashville immediately welcomed her after just one phone call, as I mentioned earlier, we knew God was up to something special. Erin assembled a small team of ladies to help her deliver and serve a fully catered meal at the club for the dancers, bouncers, bartenders, and managers.

A few times people have asked me where in the club they set up the meal. I'm always tempted to say something like, "When you are walking toward the back of the club, have you noticed the red door on the left, just before you get to the third stripper pole? They set up in there." Instead I smile and say, "Wouldn't you prefer that as a pastor I have no idea how the interior of the strip club is laid out?" The truth is, the team worked out the logistics somehow, and I don't know (or want to know) the details. Erin continued delivering meals once a month, building relationships with the dancers and managers and other employees, and asking them if there was anything she could be praying with them about.

She was soon able to connect with a national organization called Strip Church that had much more experience with this

> "Because you are valuable to God and you are valuable to me. And I just wanted to be sure you knew it."

exact type of ministry. Erin went to a training conference they hosted and came back with tons of ideas. The biggest new idea was incredibly simple: start displaying God's love at a whole new level by bringing gifts, in addition to the meal she was already providing. She had built up a Facebook group that was praying regularly for her ministry. When she asked them to pray that she could get items to take as gifts for the twenty-five dancers each time she went, the group decided to step up and be the answer to her prayer. One of the first responders was a Mary Kay rep who brought her twenty-five beauty supply kits worth $150 each. This was just the type of extravagant gift Erin had prayed for.

When she showed up at the club with the kits, the girls were overwhelmed. One girl in particular came to Erin with tears in her eyes. She wanted to know why. "I know how much these kits are worth," Katie said. "Why would you give everybody here something so valuable?"

Erin replied: "Because you are valuable to God and you are valuable to me. And I just wanted to be sure you knew it." Erin wasn't just talking about love with her words. She was authenticating it with her actions. She was loving the girls not just with her words, but with actions and in truth. The reputation she established through *showing* God's love gave her credibility when she began to *tell* Katie about God's love.

We often think of love as a feeling. But Jesus didn't command us to simply *feel* a certain way. He told us to *demonstrate* love. He didn't just *say* to love people—He *modeled* it for us in the way He lived, and even in the way He died. With people spitting on Him, mocking Him, and nailing Him to a cross,

He demonstrated love. It was a choice that led to action. Love is always a choice. And it always leads to action.

You and I can choose to demonstrate love even when our feelings aren't what they should be. Erin's initial plan with the beauty kits was to take only one or two of the items from the kits to the girls each month. After all, the kits were worth $150 each! Her feelings told her the girls wouldn't appreciate it if they got all that stuff at once. Besides, taking only a few items each time would help to ensure that she had enough gifts to last for several months. Erin finally admitted to herself, though, that deep down the reason she didn't want to give it all away at once was because she wasn't sure the girls were worth such an extravagant gift. Then she remembered God had given her an extravagant gift that she didn't deserve. So she decided to love the girls the way Jesus had loved her—extravagantly and unconditionally.

Doing this type of outreach gets messy at times. Sometimes we encounter situations where it's hard to think of a biblical example that corresponds neatly

Without love, outreach methods become nothing more than marketing gimmicks.

JOBLESS
HOMELESS
PLEASE HELP

with the specific issue we find ourselves dealing with. When that happens, it can be tough to know the right way to respond. But we have discovered a simple question that helps to cut through the fog and keeps us on track in every case: *What is the most loving thing to do in this situation?* This clarifying question is powerful because it is rooted in what Jesus said is most important: loving God and loving others. Asking this question is a simple and effective way to remind ourselves to be who we're supposed to be. It gives us a chance to pause and identify the best option, and then make the right choice.

For love to become our primary reputation, we need to be asking ourselves dozens of times every day, "What is the most loving thing I can do right now?" We can choose to process every response we make through this filter. It works in every situation. When I'm watching TV with my family and decide I'm ready for some popcorn, I can ask myself whether it's more loving to con my kids into getting it for me *or* to go myself and offer to get some for everyone else. When I notice someone taking groceries back out of her cart because she can't afford them all, I can ask whether it's more loving to mind my own business and not get involved *or* to step up and pay for her groceries. When someone posts a critical comment on Facebook that is just specific enough that his friends know whom he's criticizing and just vague enough that he can deny it, is it more loving for me to encourage him to deal with the issue privately, rather than publicly (Matt. 18:15) *or* to choose to not risk upsetting him and do nothing? This simple question consistently demands that we take action.

The question also points us toward taking the right action. For example, if I find out that someone is out of work and having trouble paying the bills, I may recognize that the most loving thing I can do is provide some financial help. I may be contacted by someone who wants help paying her bills. If this is a recurring pattern that isn't changing, I may recognize that the most loving thing I can do is to *not* help financially, but to offer to help her find ways to lower her expenses or increase her income. The most loving thing to do varies by situation.

Before you can reach people, you have to truly love them.

When it comes to evangelism, the most loving thing you can do is share the gospel by showing and telling. Without love, outreach methods become nothing more than marketing gimmicks. Before you can reach people, you have to truly love them. This kind of authentic love stemming from your relationship with God will show up in your actions, because your love is always ultimately reflected in what you do (or don't do). When your starting point is love, the goal isn't necessarily to get people to come to your church. The goal is for people to take the next step toward God. Everything else is secondary.

So what would it look like in your world if you really started loving people the way Jesus has loved you? If your reputation was love, how might that influence where you hang out and who you spend your time with? If you had processed every choice through the filter of "What is the most loving thing to do here?" what would you have done differently today? The early church was sold out to meeting needs and showing kindness to their community, and God used them to change the world. I'm convinced that if we would start focusing more on loving as Jesus loved than endlessly dissecting what He said, God could use us to change the world again.

A VERY SPECIAL EGG HUNT

By asking ourselves the question about what is the most loving thing to do as a church, we stumbled into one of my favorite outreach projects ever. At Friendship we have a huge annual event called the Great Easter Bash. It is the conclusion to our Servolution Week, where we work together as a church to invest thousands of hours into pouring out God's love in our community for the seven days before Easter.[2] This particular event has grown larger each year, so now we reserve the biggest park in our area and fill it with dozens of inflatables, pony rides, face painting, free cotton candy and popcorn, and the biggest egg hunts in the area. It is tons of fun, and thousands of people attend every year as we demonstrate God's love for our community, with no strings attached. Many of the people who make a profession of faith in Christ at our church point back to the Easter Bash as a pivotal moment that God used to cause them to want to take the next step. The event itself has grown so large that a few years ago our city decided to stop sponsoring its own event and designated ours as the "official" egg hunt (which allows those tax dollars to be used elsewhere).

Bigger isn't always better, though. We recognized that with the swelled crowds and packed parking lots, kids with special needs weren't able to enjoy the day. Sometimes our handicapped parking would fill up, which meant it was more difficult for these kids to even get there. When the egg hunt would begin, it was hard for these kids to compete with those who were faster, so they didn't get many eggs for their baskets. The lines for the other attractions were sometimes long, so most of these special kids either left discouraged or stayed home altogether. When we realized the situation, we asked ourselves, "What is the most loving thing to do here?"

Besides launching other events that we now do specifically for kids with special needs, we decided to have a completely separate Easter Bash just for them. We do it a week before the big Bash. We rent out the same park and have most of the same attractions, but everything is tailored just for children with disabilities.

The coolest part is probably the egg hunt. We partner each kid with a volunteer "buddy" to assist him or her during the hunt. The parents love having the buddy, because it frees them up to be able to take pictures and enjoy watching their kid have a blast, rather than having to attend to every minor detail with their child. While we have age-graded hunts for most of the kids, our team got really creative with specialized hunts for those with visual impairments and mobility limitations. For the visually impaired hunt, we have special oversized plastic eggs that have blinking red lights and make a beeping sound. Since there aren't thousands of people everywhere, the kids are able to both hear the beeps and see the blinking lights to find the eggs all by themselves. For those with wheelchairs or walkers, we use normal plastic eggs and tape a small steel hex nut to the inside of each egg. We then give each of the kids a magnetic retrieving baton (the kind a mechanic would use). When they come to an egg, they just reach out and touch it with the baton. Because of the hex nut inside, the egg sticks to the end of the magnetic baton. Then they can just remove the egg from the baton and put it in their basket. This allows some of these kids to do an egg hunt without assistance for the first time in their lives.

I cannot begin to tell you all of the positive comments we get from these families. They are so appreciative, not only that there is a community event just for them, but that we strive to do it with as much excellence as the big Bash. One mom of a child with autism told me, "It's just great to be in a public setting where, when my child takes off running, nobody looks at me like, 'What is wrong with you?' Everybody here just knows there's an issue and that it's okay." Our volunteers are now completely addicted to serving these special families with Christ's love and seeing their faces light up. I think we almost enjoy it even more than they do.

When you ask yourself what is the most loving thing to do in a situation, and then do it, it may cost you time and energy and money, but it is always worth it. When you step up and demon-strate selfless love, you are building exactly the relationship Jesus wants you to have.

YOUR REPUTATION ISN'T WHAT YOU THINK IT IS

My fear is that you are reading this and thinking all of this talk about being more loving is good information that will hopefully benefit someone else. Since you are already a loving person, though, it doesn't really apply to you. So let's deal with that.

The fact is, you really are a loving person. All of your friends would describe you that way. There is probably not anybody who would say you are overtly unloving. So since your friends like you and no one hates you, is that the same thing as having a reputation for being loving? Are you really known for how you love?

Jesus said, "Listen, what's the big deal if you love people who already love you? Even scoundrels do that much!" (Luke 6:32). God made us in such a way that we all naturally love certain people. I had a boss once who was so gruff and who cussed so much that I wondered if it was possible for him to love anybody. But I realized even this grumpy guy loved his family and closest friends. He was just really bad at showing it. Some of us think we are incredibly loving people because we have certain friends and family members we care about, while we're actually only doing what every other human does. Even scoundrels do that much.

When I married Erin, I pledged to love her "for better or for worse." When she is really on her game and we're having a "for better" day, it is easy to show my love for her. On the "for worse" days, when she is in a bad mood (hypothetically speaking, since this has never actually happened), let's just say it is a little bit more of a challenge to be as kind as on the good days. Some days it is effortless for me to express love, and other days it is just plain hard. I am sure she would say the same about me. But if I let my circumstances dictate my response, then my reputation will be that I am moody and inconsistent. The only way I can build a reputation for being loving is by showing love when it does not come naturally. If I'm going to be known for love, then even when I am in a hurry or having a bad hair day, I have to choose to demonstrate love, especially for hard-to-love people.

Every person I've talked with about this is under the impression that he or she is known as a loving person. There is a problem with that self-appraisal. You don't get to decide whether you're known as loving. By definition, your reputation isn't about what you think at all. It is determined by what *other* people think. It gets decided by your community. It doesn't really matter whether you agree or disagree with their assessment. The goal isn't for you to *think* you are loving. The goal is to be *known* by other people as loving. So if you aren't satisfied with what your reputation in your community is currently, then you will have to start going above and beyond to change it.

Your reputation is determined by what *other* people think.

You can't afford to miss this point, so I'll be blunt. *If people aren't already describing you as loving, then it is because you aren't.* The same can be said for your church. If your community isn't already describing your church as loving, then it isn't. This doesn't mean that if we surveyed people in your neighborhood, most of them would not describe you as loving. Here's the deal: when you or your church has a real reputation for loving like Jesus, you'll overhear your community talking about it. Christlike love is so different from what people normally experience that it stands out and they take notice. They can't help but tell their friends about it, and they will even tell you about it.

This past Sunday, a lady pulled her car into the edge of our parking lot and stopped. She got out of the car and approached one of our parking attendants with some money in her hand. She said, "I keep hearing about this church and seeing what you guys are doing all over the place. I'm so excited and I want to be a part. I just got finished with a night shift, though, so I'm going to bed. But I wanted to go ahead this week and give an offering to support the church, and I'll be here next week." I love when those kinds of thing happen, because it confirms that we're building the reputation Jesus said we should have.

In fact, we now have as many people come to check out Friendship as first-time guests because they *heard* about the way we love, as we do people whom we actually directly reached out to and served. That's the power of a reputation for loving people. When you show kindness to others, not only will you get to point the people you serve toward God, but you sometimes even get to be a Christlike example for the people who simply heard about your kindness.

Church leaders: Is your community talking about how loving you are? I'm not talking about whether you have a food pantry or sometimes go on mission trips. Mission trips are great, but when a church has a better reputation with people two thousand miles away than it does with the guy living right down the street, then that is a problem. If your love isn't surfacing in tangible ways by meeting needs around you and lifting people toward becoming who God intended them to be, then it isn't the kind of love Jesus demonstrated. Love can't just be another thing we do. It has to be the *primary* thing we do because it is not just what we do, but who we are.

I DON'T LIKE YOU, AND I DON'T THINK GOD IS CRAZY ABOUT YOU EITHER

Before I went into ministry, I don't think I had any enemies. As far as I know, everyone who knew me basically liked me. I got along with everybody from lawyers to rednecks to Dallas Cowboys fans. Then I became a preacher boy and devoted my life to helping people connect with Jesus and experience more of the abundant life He intended for them to have. I thought people would be so appreciative of what I was doing, they would circle "pastor appreciation month" on their calendars and eagerly count down the days until they could shower me with gratitude. By the way, the designated month for that is October, just in case you weren't sure how many shopping days you had left.

Boy, was I wrong about how people were going to react. I was shocked the first time I found out that some people I had thought were my biggest supporters were gossiping about me and criticizing me. They said things about me that weren't true and seemed to assume the worst about me. Some of it was silly and some of it was hurtful. One rumor they started was that I was "in it for the money" and got a financial bonus for every person that was baptized. If that were true, I'd probably start baptizing pets just to inflate the numbers. One family started trashing me because I didn't come to their relative's funeral. When they told the story, they left out the part about how they never told me anyone had died. I got really depressed and thought it couldn't get any worse than having people talk about me behind my back. Then they started criticizing me right to my face. I decided I had liked it better when they did it behind my back.

Jesus faced more than His fair share of criticism. His first followers knew a thing or two about being harassed. The early church got more bad publicity than Lance Armstrong. But even as they dealt with an avalanche of negativity, they won over more and more people, and the movement of Christ followers grew exponentially because people were magnetically drawn toward their love. It was authentic and undeniable. It showed up in the way they treated each other, in how they reacted to needs in the community, and even in their response to their enemies.

John wrote: "If someone claims, 'I love God,' but hates his brother or sister, then he is a liar. Anyone who does not love a brother or sister, whom he has seen, cannot possibly love God, whom he has never seen" (1 John 4:20).

I can easily convince myself I'm a loving person. After all, I always have good intentions, I buy the newspaper from the guys with the homeless ministry at least once a week, and sometimes when I'm criticized, I can successfully keep my mouth shut. I had thought that was enough. Besides, even if there were a few people I secretly hated, I was sure I could still have an awesome relationship with God. Then John had to go and drop that bomb. Thanks, John.

Here is the principle in what John is saying: I really only love God as much as I love the person whom I love the least.[3] No matter how loving I may think I am, I can get an accurate gauge of my heart for God by measuring what is the least amount of love I have for somebody else. John said I cannot have more love for the God whom I have not seen than I do for this person I don't care to ever see again. Was John saying that my love for the person who criticized me and tried to undermine my ministry sets the limit on how much love I actually have for God? Yep, that was exactly what he was saying.

So what about you? Who would head your personal list of the top ten most unlovable people you know? Maybe it is the person who publicly embarrassed you on Facebook. Or your ex-spouse. Or the kid who stole your lunch money when you were in third grade. And definitely the punk who bullied your own kid in third grade.

> I really only love God as much as I love the person whom I love the least.

Our love for our enemies becomes the ceiling on our love for God. It also determines how much of a reputation for love we'll have and, in turn, how effectively we'll be able to share God's love with others, because as I said earlier, people will have a hard time believing God loves them if they're positive we don't.

This truth has caused me to recalibrate my entire approach to outreach. I've realized that the homosexual activist isn't the enemy. Neither is the Muslim. The strippers and porn producers aren't my enemies either. They are who I'm supposed to love. They are the mission field. I'm fairly certain they are who Jesus would spend lots of time with if He were walking the planet today. Since He is the one we're following, this means we have got to spend time with these people too. The only way you are ever going to love people who are unlike you is if you start spending time with them. When you do, it won't take long before you realize they really have become your friends. Every time you develop a friendship with someone who is so dissimilar to you, I think it causes Jesus to smile because those were exactly the types of people He hung out with.

I know what you're thinking. *If I get serious about reaching out to these kinds of people and start investing in their lives, some of my church friends might misunderstand. If I really accept them and start spending time with people like that, other people may see my kindness and compassion and assume I am endorsing and approving of everything they do.* You're exactly right. That is probably going to happen. People are probably going to misconstrue what you're doing and put a label on you that you don't want. Welcome to the footsteps of Jesus. He was misunderstood and criticized for the exact same thing, so at least you'll be in good company.

I wish I could tell you it will all work out great and that everyone else at your church will be just as excited about showing God's love to these people whom most churches have excluded for far too long. It's probably going to be a bumpy ride, though. Jesus loved everybody perfectly, and yet the religious people hated Him. So brace yourself. You're probably not going to do this nearly as well as He did, so not everybody is going to understand what you are doing either. Just remember that popular opinion wasn't what motivated Jesus, so it can't be the determining factor for how we do outreach either. Do whatever it takes to start building a reputation as the most loving person around. You just might be the catalyst God uses to re-brand how your community sees Him.

DISCUSSION QUESTIONS

- Of all the characteristics and qualities Jesus could have selected as the key identifier of a disciple, why do you think He chose love?

- Why do you think some people want to make spiritual maturity more about how much you know than about how well you love?

- Is it possible to think you are a rather loving person, while at the same time the people who are closest to you don't feel very loved by you?

- If almost everyone understands that love is important *and* almost everyone wants to be known as a loving person, then why aren't expressions of love more common?

- What are the benefits of having a me-first attitude?

- How would it benefit *you* to be a more loving person to *others*?

- If the person you love the least sets the limit on how much love you have for God, then how much love do you currently have for God?

- If you had processed every choice through the filter of "What is the most loving thing to do here?" what would you have done differently today?

- As you begin to take steps to build a reputation for loving others, what are you going to *do* differently next week?

MEET THEM WHERE THEY ARE

To invite people to move toward God from where they are, make it safe for them to explore their next step.

We have two different Buffalo Wild Wings locations within five miles of our house. I sometimes think this must be similar to what heaven will be like. It is a great feeling to know I am never more than a few minutes away from hot wings and dozens of television screens showing every conceivable sporting event. Erin insists that when I say, "hot wings," I should clarify I actually mean mild wings that are almost dry because there is so little sauce. The honest truth is anything spicier than that makes me sweat like crazy. Evidently my tolerance for buffalo sauce is roughly equivalent to that of a six-year-old girl. But I love the taste, so I keep getting hot (aka "mild") wings, even though the servers usually laugh at me as I down glass after glass of water to stay cooled off.

Not long ago, Erin sent me a text to meet her and the kids at the restaurant at 6:00. I got there right on time and got a table for us. I started watching a ball game and before I knew it, ten minutes had passed. Erin usually lets me know when she is running late, so I was a little perturbed that she hadn't bothered to notify me. When another five minutes passed and there was no still sign of them, I started getting downright irritated. About that time, my phone rang. As soon as I answered, Erin said, "Where are you?"

"What do you mean, where am I? I'm where you're supposed to be! Why aren't you here?" (While my words seem harsh in print, I am pretty sure I said them in the most loving, encouraging, and gentle way possible.)

Erin said, "I'm at the Buffalo Wild Wings I told you to be at. Maybe you should read your text again." That was when I realized I was at the wrong location. So now I had a choice to make. Would I stick to my guns, stay where I was, and eat alone? Or would I swallow my pride, admit I was in the wrong place, and go to where they were? Since I have lots of practice at admitting my mistakes because I make them every day, I apologized to my server for the confusion

Maybe we should occasionally pack up, head out, and meet people where they are.

and headed out to meet them. It was really the only logical thing to do.

When it comes to outreach, we face the exact same decision, but inexplicably often don't make the obvious choice. I frequently talk with people who have a heart for reaching out and who want to see their community connect with God's love. They sometimes don't understand why more new people aren't showing up at their church or small group meetings. In some cases, they have even spent quite a bit of money trying to get people to come to their meeting spot. It is as if the thought never occurs to them that since people aren't coming to their location, maybe they should occasionally pack up, head out, and meet them where they are.

PAUL WAS ANYTHING BUT A SELL-OUT

Every time I read through the book of Acts, I am amazed at all that Paul accomplished in his lifetime. His capacity for reaching new people in new areas with the gospel is astounding. He started new churches in some of the most culturally diverse locations imaginable. Within those new churches, he was able to get people who were very dissimilar to work together—Jews and Gentiles, men and women, rich and poor, slaves and masters. Not only was he able to successfully launch these churches in areas that had never previously even heard the gospel, but he quickly built them up to the point that they were sustainable without him so he could move on to the next area to reach others.

In his letter to the church at Corinth, he elaborated on his strategy.

I am free of obligations to all people. And, even though no one *(except Jesus)* owns me, I have become a slave *by my own free will* to everyone *in hopes* that I would gather more *believers.* When around Jews, I emphasize my Jewishness in order to win them over. When around those who live *strictly* under the law, I live by its regulations—even though I have a different perspective on the law now—in order to win them over. *In the same way,* I've made a life outside the law to gather those who live outside the law (although I personally abide by and live under the Anointed One's law). I've been *broken, lost, depressed, oppressed, and* weak that I might *find favor and gain the weak.* I'm *flexible, adaptable, and* able to do and be whatever is needed for all kinds of people so that *in the end* I can use every means at my disposal to offer them salvation. (1 Cor. 9:19–22)

To understand Paul's point, we have to first recognize that he was a Jew. He basically said, "If I'm around Jews and I need to emphasize my Jewishness by swapping matzo ball soup recipes and talking about how awesome Barbra Streisand is, then I'll do it. Why? Because I'll do whatever it takes to win them over."

> **Paul would be whoever people needed him to be.**

If he was dealing with experts in the law, then he could quote the law to them (since he would have memorized it as a student). He could use the law as the starting point to show them how Jesus was the fulfillment of the law. But since he no longer lived under the regulations of the law, he could relate just as easily to those who knew nothing about the law. When he was dealing with hurting people, he could find common ground because of the trials he had faced through experiencing shipwrecks, being beaten, and running for his life. He would be whoever they needed him to be.

Today if we were to hear someone say he was trying to be all things to all people, we would probably accuse him of being a sell-out. We'd say, "You don't seem to know who you are. You're not consistent. You're wishy-washy. You change how you act and how you present yourself based on whomever you're with."

Paul would respond to our allegation, "That is exactly right. I'll change my approach, my language, my habits, and whatever else about me needs to change to remove any unnecessary barriers between me and the person I'm trying to reach. What I never change is my goal of doing whatever it takes to connect with people, because the central message of Jesus' love never changes." Paul ultimately wasn't concerned with what people thought about him. Like a chameleon, he would be whoever they needed him to be to allow them to see Jesus clearly.

WHO ARE WE TRYING TO RELATE TO?

Missionaries in foreign countries instinctively take the same approach as Paul. They adapt to the culture they're in. They allow the people's local customs and preferences to influence the type of building their church meets in, the way they dress, the style of music they play and sing, their teaching methods, and obviously the language they speak. It's not that the missionaries don't necessarily have a favorite teaching style or a personal inclination about how they might otherwise dress if they were back in the States. But their overriding goal is to connect people with Christ. So they suppress their own preferences because they want to make sure they don't create any unnecessary barriers between the people they are trying to reach and the unchanging message of the gospel.

When Erin and I invite guests over to our house, we act differently than we do when it's just family. Since we have three boys ages thirteen and under, we have established some basic guidelines that go into effect whenever we have company. We have to all make sure we close the bathroom door when we're in there, we don't make or imitate bodily function sounds at the table, and we don't reenact Michael Jackson videos wearing only our boxers. That last guideline was implemented more to keep me in check than anything the kids are likely to do. We restrict ourselves in these ways because we want our guests to be comfortable while they are in our home. In Paul's letter to the church at Corinth, he talked specifically about how important it was that they be aware of first-time guests when they meet for worship. As he wrote to the church about their practice of speaking in tongues, he said, "If you speak a word of blessing in the spirit only, then how will an uninformed person who can't understand your prayer say 'Amen' when you are done giving thanks? Even though you give thanks *to God* well, the unknowing person doesn't benefit" (1 Cor. 14:16–17). He encouraged the church to remember that there were outsiders showing up at their meetings who didn't yet understand everything. So he wanted the church to restrict

> **Becoming more culturally relevant doesn't make a church less biblical: it makes it *more* biblical.**

themselves so they could meet their guests where they were, rather than just ignoring or confusing them. If we're going to reach out and invite people to move toward God from where they are, then it's important that we do all we can to make it safe for them to explore their next step.

Years ago, when Friendship was still in the planning stages, I wrestled with this idea of a church being culturally relevant. I was concerned it would be a compromise to allow the culture to shape our approach to outreach. It felt as if we would be trying to be all things to all people and that I was rejecting things about the church and the traditions I had grown up with. When I finally began to understand the implications of what Paul said and did to reach people, it was as if a lightbulb turned on inside my head. Becoming more culturally relevant doesn't make a church less biblical: it makes it *more* biblical. It means doing what Paul did by being "*flexible, adaptable, and* able to do and be whatever is needed for all kinds of people so that *in the end* [we] can use every means at [our] disposal to offer them salvation" (1 Cor. 9:22). So my job and your job is to take the unchanging message of God's love and allow our constantly changing culture to influence how we express it.

NOBODY WANTS TO BE MR. IRRELEVANT

Each year in the NFL draft, the player selected with the very last pick receives a dubious honor: Mr. Irrelevant. The main perk of this title is getting to attend the Irrelevant Week festivities in California, where he receives his trophy. The award mimics the Heisman Trophy, except that the player on this trophy is fumbling the football. While getting drafted in the NFL is definitely a good thing, Mr. Irrelevant's odds of making the team are fairly low. In most cases, he would probably have a better chance at success if he went undrafted. Since undrafted players can still be invited to team training camps, being a "free agent" would allow him to try out for the team he thinks is most likely to add someone to its roster who plays his position, rather than being locked in with the team that drafted him.

If you're going to be effective in reaching out, then you don't want to be Mr. Irrelevant either. Being relevant means putting aside your own preferences and putting someone else's first. Deferring to someone else's first choice is a practical way you can serve that person. Paul encouraged the Christians at Philippi to do this very thing: "Don't let selfishness and prideful agendas take over. Embrace true humility, and lift your heads to extend love to others. Get beyond yourselves and protecting your own interests; *be sincere*, and secure your neighbors' interests first. *In other words,* adopt the mind-set of Jesus the Anointed" (Phil. 2:3–5).

Unfortunately, selfishness is one of the hardest things to see in the mirror, and that is what causes us to be irrelevant. Almost nobody thinks they aren't connecting with the people around them. That is because the people with whom we spend the most time probably have most of the same preferences and opinions as us. That is probably one of the reasons we like spending time with them. If anyone doesn't like the same things the same way we do, then we can dismiss him as either having a wrong opinion or bad taste. We don't think of our opinions as "selfishness and prideful agendas," but as Paul said, they can become selfish if we are unwilling to "get beyond" ourselves and put our "neighbors' interests first."

Since everybody has different tastes, we can safely say that everything is relevant to somebody. Some people love hour-long lectures that drill down on the etymology of words and the nuances of ancient verb tenses, while others can focus for about fifteen minutes, and then they need a commercial break. Some people wouldn't dream of missing a Gaither Homecoming Tour, while others prefer more contemporary styles of music. There are even some people in the world who once bought a ticket to a Milli Vanilli concert. (I'm still not sure what I paid for at that "live" concert, since it turned out they were lip-synching the whole time.) Some people spend their time at church functions, while others go to strip clubs. The question is, if our goal is to help people who don't know God to connect with Him, then whose culture are we trying to relate to? Are you "protecting your own interests" and trying to get people to switch to your preferences, or will you get beyond yourself and defer to theirs? Paul chose to be culturally relevant to the people he was trying to reach—whether Jew or Gentile, legalist or libertarian, strong or weak.

Everything is relevant to somebody.

I was contacted once by a small church that, in their own words, was dying. Their attendance had dwindled to a handful of people, so they wanted an outside perspective on their situation and some input as to what they should do next. As I met with these church leaders, I was struggling to get them to understand the importance of making changes to meet people where they are. So I finally asked them, "What would you *not* be willing to change even if it absolutely meant that more people would be reached with the gospel? I'm not saying I have a silver bullet that is guaranteed to do anything. I just want to be clear about what is off-limits. So what are you *not* willing to change, even if you were 100 percent certain that the change would cause more people to be reached for Christ?"

They discussed the question for a few minutes and offered up a few things they simply felt were out of bounds and could not imagine ever changing. I told them, "The only acceptable answer to that question is 'Nothing.' There can't be *anything* you're not willing to do or change if it means more people would be reached. You can never compromise the message of the gospel, and you certainly don't sin to reach people. But outside of that, you have to be willing to do whatever it takes to reach people. Otherwise, you've forgotten your purpose as a church."

When a farmer goes out to plant a seed, there is only so much he can do that day.

Perhaps you're thinking, *Yeah, churches like that need to be willing to change.* If you are, then you've missed the point. YOU need to be willing to change. You have your own opinions and tastes. You have places you like to hang out and a type of person you prefer to spend time with. If you're unwilling to defer to the preferences of the people you're trying to reach, then you are creating an unnecessary barrier that could prevent people from seeing God's love through your life. Are there things you're unwilling to do to demonstrate God's love? Are there places you're unwilling to go? I can promise you that spending Thursday nights at a strip club wasn't always Erin's preference, but she humbled herself so she could connect with the people she hoped to reach.

ONE STEP AT A TIME

Remember, when Paul said he was striving to be all things to all people so he could win them over, he wasn't talking about how to "do church." He was talking about how he personally did outreach. In that same letter to the Corinthian church, he reminded them that when he had first met them and begun the church in Corinth, he had met them where they were. He said, "I planted the seed, Apollos watered it, but God has been making it grow" (1 Cor. 3:6 NIV).

Paul had given them what they were ready for at the time he was with them. Then Apollos came along and took them a little further. Paul wanted them to stop arguing about which teacher was more important, because they were working together for a common cause. Both Paul and Apollos had done their part by ushering the people to take the next step toward becoming more like Christ. God was the One who deserved all the credit because He was the One enabling them to continue to grow, step-by-step.

With outreach, we tend to get hyper-focused on the harvest. We can sometimes forget that planting the seed is just as important. When a farmer goes out to plant a seed, there is only so much he can do that day. He certainly doesn't expect to go out in the morning to plant seeds, and then come home that evening with a load of vegetables. It takes time for the seed to grow. He does what he can to give the seed every chance to germinate and develop, and then trusts God to do what he can't do—like providing rain and sunshine. When the conditions are right and the vegetables and fruit are finally mature and ready, it's a beautiful thing.

After Erin had been reaching out to workers at the strip club for several months, she began taking gifts for them, in addition to the fully catered meal she already brought each time. It was this tangible expression of God's love that caught Katie's attention. As a single mom of two who was trying to make ends meet by dancing at the club, she didn't have time for games. Erin didn't judge her or preach at her. She lovingly invited Katie to take a next step by coming to church with her. She even offered to treat her and her kids to lunch after the worship service.

Several weeks later, Katie decided to check out Friendship on a Sunday. On her way to church that morning, she got in a minor traffic accident with another car. It turned out that the other person in the wreck was also on her way to Friendship. So she stood on the side of the road and heard all about this church that was focused on finding practical ways to show God's love for everybody. By the time she finally arrived that morning, the worship experience was concluding with a baptism celebration. As Katie watched people publicly thank God for giving them a second chance, she decided maybe it was possible for her to experience a second chance too. The following Sunday, she asked God to be the new boss of her life and to forgive her for the things she had done wrong, pledged to follow His plan, and trusted that Jesus' death on the cross had made it possible for her to be right with God.

> **Everything she said would have been absolutely true and absolutely wrong.**

A couple of days later, Erin was preparing for another visit to the strip club. She called Katie to ask whether she'd be there working that night. Katie told her she had realized this job wasn't part of God's plan for her life. She had already quit the lucrative job, even though she now wasn't sure how she would be able to pay the bills. She said she was trusting God to take care of her and that she was "ready to feel beautiful again." This girl had been a Christian for two days and was already taking steps of faith bigger than some churchgoers take in their entire lives. We immediately got a human resources rep in our church involved and helped get her connected to a new job. It wasn't a great job, but it would pay the bills for now.

Erin and Katie's friendship continued to grow. Erin quickly became not just a friend to Katie, but a mentor. Katie continued taking steps and growing in her faith, and God was showing up in her life in remarkable ways. After she had been following Christ for a couple of months, she started dating a new guy. Erin recognized it was time to invite her to take another step. She said, "I don't know whether anyone has ever told you this, but God's plan for you is to not have sex again until you're married. It's the best investment you can make in your future marriage, and it's in the best interest of you and your kids. God isn't trying to prevent you from enjoying life. He gives you that boundary because He loves you."

> We simply make it our goal to invite people to take the *next* step toward Christ from wherever they are.

Katie said, "I've never dated anyone more than three weeks without sleeping with him. It's hard to imagine saving myself from now until I'm married." She shared how past events had left her feeling like "damaged goods," and she wasn't even sure she was worth saving herself for marriage. What she said next was so beautiful that it still brings tears to my eyes. She decided, "I've trusted God and already seen Him show up in so many ways, how could I not trust Him in this? I'm all in."

A couple of months later, Katie told Erin, "I've been thinking. Most of the clothes I wear really aren't very appropriate. I thought about donating them to Goodwill for a tax deduction, but then I realized that would just mean someone else would be wearing them. So I'm just going to burn them." This wasn't an issue anyone had mentioned or specifically pointed out. She had simply realized on her own this was the next step in her journey of becoming more Christlike, and she took it. So you had better believe we went into action and made sure she got some gift cards very soon to help her take that step and buy a new wardrobe.

Here is my point with this story. If Erin had gone into the strip club and told Katie and the others, "You need to stop having sex outside of marriage and burn all of your clothes," how many people would she have reached? Not only would her relationship with Katie have ended right there, but Erin would have been told she wasn't welcome at the club anymore. If Erin had said those things to Katie that night, then everything she said would have been absolutely true and absolutely wrong. It would have been wrong for Erin to start there because those weren't Katie's next steps. Erin needed to meet her right where she was, and then lovingly invite her to take the next step from there.

I'M HOPING YOU'LL SAY YOU DON'T KNOW IF THERE IS A GOD

There's an ancient Chinese saying that a journey of a thousand miles begins with the first step. I've always thought a long journey began with a visit to Expedia.com and a lot of luggage. Author James Engel published an idea in 1973 about communicating the gospel to others in a way that takes into account the journey people are on and the next step they need to take.[1] He created a numeric scale, where everyone falls somewhere on the scale in terms of how receptive they are to the gospel and where they are in the decision-making process. Here's a modified version of his original chart.

−10	No God framework	"Who is God?"
−9	Atheist: denies existence of God and supernatural	"There's no such thing as God."
−8	Agnostic: not sure it's possible to know if there is a God	"I'm just not sure."
−7	Al-Anon view of God: vague belief in God; aware of Jesus	"I think there's a higher power."
−6	Interested in Jesus/Christianity; perhaps used to attend a church; open to finding out more	"There might be something to this."
−5	Has personally experienced Christian love; wants to find out more	"Why would someone do something so selfless for me?"
−4	Aware of the basic facts of the gospel; attends church	"I'll kick the tires and see if there might be something to Christianity."
−3	Aware of own personal need for Jesus, whether for forgiveness or a new direction in life	"I've not always done what God wanted me to do."
−2	Grasps the implications of what Jesus did	"It's not about being good enough: it's about what Jesus did on the cross for me."
−1	Challenged to respond personally	"I need to turn away from sin and to God. I need Him to forgive me and take charge of my life."
0	Repents and puts faith in Christ	"God is now the boss of my life. I'm trusting and following His plan."

+1	Baptized	"I'm identifying with Christ's death, burial, and resurrection."
+2	Becomes active member of local church	"I'm connecting with other followers and doing life with them."
+3	Continues to grow in character, service, and relationships	"I'm spending time with God, serving others, and becoming more Christlike."
+4	Leads others to connect with Christ and take next steps	"I'm reaching out and inviting others to take their own next step toward God."

Let me explain the concept behind this chart. Everyone is somewhere on this scale, depending on his or her current view of and relationship with God. In theory, people will tend to move through the scale in a linear fashion. In reality, people will sometimes take three steps forward and then two steps back. Sometimes they might move through multiple stages on the scale in a very short time, perhaps even in just a few moments. Other times people will take years before they move from one stage to the next. Sometimes, they get stuck and never go any further. Perhaps you can think of other sub-stages not listed on the chart. You may even want to switch the list around because you feel the steps should be listed in a different order. That's okay. This isn't a perfect model. Regardless, I think we can agree with the big idea that this scale is overall a fair representation of where people are spiritually and the steps they generally go through in their spiritual journey.

Here is how this concept can impact our approach to outreach. We simply make it our goal to invite people to take the *next* step toward Christ from wherever they are. Let's consider an example. I'm not sure I've ever encountered anyone in America who has never heard of God at all (−10), so let's assume we're talking with someone we would categorize as −9 on the scale. My aim with an atheist is to encourage her to at least take the next step, which on this scale would mean she decides, "I'm just not sure whether there is a God or not." With this understanding of evangelism, this would mean she is moving toward God. The way I see it, that is a win.

So think for a moment about the implications of this approach. Am I saying that someone could say she is not even sure there is a God, and I would consider that a good thing? If I'm reaching out to an atheist, then that is exactly what I'm saying. In fact, hearing her say that would be a reason to celebrate. I am thrilled when that happens because this is the next step toward God from where she was.

We're just recognizing the fact that seeds don't germinate and produce fruit in a day.

Could God radically save an atheist in a single day? Of course! With God all things are possible. By inviting people to take the next step from where they are, we're not limiting what God *could* do. We're simply recognizing that people are at different points on their spiritual journeys and we are choosing to meet them where they are, rather than assuming they should already be where we want them to be.

I can hear someone objecting and saying, "But shouldn't we be calling them to repent of their sins and surrender their lives to Christ?" Of course that is the ultimate goal! We're just recognizing the fact that seeds don't germinate and produce fruit in a day. It's a process that takes time. If you're married, then you probably didn't have a wedding on the same day you first met your spouse. You needed some time to get to know each other, to find out whether you could trust each other, and perhaps most impor- tant, to make sure you both agreed that Jar Jar Binks was an epic mistake in the *Star Wars* movies. If it took time for us to decide to make a lifetime commitment to a person, shouldn't we expect it will often take time for a person to make an eternal commitment to God?

For whatever reason, we tend to think of discipleship and evangelism as two completely separate things. The Engel Scale shows how they are both part of the same spiritual-growth process of moving toward Christ. Everyone can agree that after a person becomes a Christian, spiritual growth is a process that takes time. Nobody expects a new believer to be immediately mature in his faith. For some reason, though, it's not always as easy to recognize that people also go through a process *before* they become Christians. Evangelism, like discipleship, is a process of moving forward one step at a time.

One thing we have done at Friendship to help new believers continue to grow and take next steps is put together a discipleship video curriculum. We created a series of ten videos, in which each ten-minute video introduces a new concept and invites the per- son to take that next step. We make the videos available online and send new believers a weekly e-mail with the link to their next video. After watching, they are invited to respond in some specific way (usually via e-mail) that lets us know they have taken the next step and are continuing to move forward. This allows us to continue to meet them where they are, rather than moving too quickly by expecting them to be somewhere else. We also have a supplemental book and small group curriculum to encourage new believers to continue growing step-by-step.

MINDI'S STORY

Erin and I sometimes invite new attenders at our church to Sunday lunch so we can get to know them better. It also gives me a good excuse to occasionally get out of helping with teardown after our worship service. Of course, when we invite people, we always pay for everyone's meal. Neil and Mindi had attended our church a couple of times when they agreed to meet us at our favorite Mexican restaurant.

We had just sat down, the complimentary chips and salsa were being delivered, and I was still taking off my coat. Mindi decided to go ahead and

When our only approach to outreach is to present the basic facts of the gospel to everyone, we're like a handyman with only one tool.

jump-start the conversation and said, "Just so you know, I'm an agnostic Jew." I wasn't sure exactly what that meant, but it would put her at a clear −8 on the Engel Scale, if you're keeping score at home. I replied, "Okay. Do you guys want some queso dip?" No one has ever started a conversation with me quite that way, so I honestly wasn't sure what else to say. She obviously knew I was a pastor, so I wasn't sure whether she wanted to shut down any talk about spiritual issues, to debate the existence of God, or to just make me aware of her position. Regardless, I thought it was wise to move on with the conversation and lunch, because I was just hoping to get to know them better and perhaps become friends. Also, I was really hungry, and I really like chips and queso dip.

Over lunch, we learned that Neil was a Christian and that he and Mindi had agreed to raise their two-year-old daughter in a Christian environment. Mindi planned to attend occasionally, but not to get too involved. We all became fast friends. The more time we spent with them, the more we liked them. Over the next few months, we did many things for them that could be described as acts of kindness (which is an invitation to −5), simply because those are the types of things we like to do for our friends. We didn't push Mindi on the faith issue, but our relationship with Christ came up naturally in conversations at times. We went to movies and sporting events, ate out (a lot), and even took a couple of trips together.

The Sunday when Neil stayed home with their sick daughter and Mindi came to church alone anyway, I knew she was moving toward Jesus. She was at least at −4 on the scale, and perhaps at step −3 or −2.

Not long afterward, she called and asked if she and Neil could come and talk with me about Christ. I said, "No way. I've got better things to do." Just kidding! I had been praying for this conversation for months, so I cleared my schedule. Mindi was our friend, so we very much wanted her to have a relationship with Jesus. We were friends whether she followed Him or not, but we knew how her life and eternity would be changed for the better if Christ were in it.

Mindi explained that she understood the gospel and now believed everything we had said about Jesus. There was only one thing holding her back: her Jewish heritage. She was afraid that embracing Jesus as her Savior would mean she was rejecting her cultural upbringing. I knew from previous things Mindi had told me that, for her, Judaism was primarily an identity and tradition, rather than a specific set of beliefs about God. That was why she originally described herself as an agnostic Jew. She was agnostic in her beliefs, but Jewish by birthright.

I explained to Mindi that Jesus didn't come to oppose the Jewish faith: He came to fulfill it. Even though she may not have personally been looking for a Messiah, God had promised one to her ancestors. Embracing Jesus wasn't a repudiation of her cultural heritage. Instead, it was recognizing that her Messiah had come. I told her that accepting Jesus was simply about repentance and faith (0 on the scale). It wasn't repentance and faith *and* her mom agreeing with her decision. It was repentance and faith alone.

Seeing Mindi respond to Christ was one of the highlights of my ministry. She could hardly wait to be baptized. She continues to grow stronger in her relationship with Jesus, has invited dozens of people to church, and participates in our servant evangelism projects on a regular basis. She told me yesterday, "I try to be more Christlike every day. I realize I still have a lot to learn, but thanks to Friendship, I am still growing." Just as she moved toward a relationship with Jesus one step at a time, she is continuing to grow step-by-step.

SOMETIMES A HAMMER IS THE WRONG TOOL

Most outreach training I have gone through has been taught from the perspective of evangelism exclusively as a transaction. The focus was on "sealing the deal" and getting people to "pray the prayer." That view made for a great approach whenever I'd come across someone who was ready to take that specific step. But whenever I'd encounter people who weren't at that point in their spiritual journeys, I didn't know what to do with them. I wasn't sure whether I should try to give them my gospel presentation again to see if it worked better the second time, or if I should just walk away and tell them to enjoy their eternal damnation in the lake of fire. Instead of aggressively pushing people to step across the line of faith today (whether they're ready for that step or not), we want to lovingly reach out to them and invite them to take the *next* step from wherever they are. That is why we call it out*reach*, rather than out*push*.

When our only approach to outreach is to present the basic facts of the gospel to everyone, we're like a handyman with only one tool. When he encounters a situation that calls for a minor adjustment with a screwdriver, he pulls out his hammer and starts pounding. Not only is his approach to solving the problem unhelpful, but it will probably make the situation worse. In fact, it might damage the screw, making it almost impossible for anyone to adjust it later, even with the right tool. There's nothing wrong with the hammer, and the handyman may be a hammer expert. The problem is that it is being used in a situation that calls for a different tool.

In the same way, when our only tool for outreach is a basic gospel presentation, we'll only be effective when we connect with people who are ready to take that specific step. If people are at any other point on their spiritual journey, then we won't have anything to offer them. We won't be able to help them take another step closer to God from any other point because we'll only know how to facilitate this one step of challenging people to respond to the gospel. Even worse, we may actually repel them farther away from God by coming across as out of touch and making the gospel seem irrelevant.

I've heard well-meaning Christians say, "But there is nothing more loving than telling people the truth. There can never be anything wrong with challenging someone to respond to the gospel." I respectfully disagree, because there is something very wrong with insensitively presenting the gospel in a way that actually pushes them *farther away* from Jesus. If I am going to be known for love, like Jesus was, then I will meet them where they are and invite them to take the next step from there. In terms of the Engel Scale, if a person is at −8, then I'm not going to be very effective in my outreach efforts if all I know how to do is talk to people who are at −1.

One of the questions every husband dreads hearing is, "Do these pants make me look fat?" If it so happens the pants are every bit as unflattering as the wife fears, then he has a choice to make. He could say, "I didn't think it was possible for those pants to make you look even fatter, but they actually do." That statement might be 100 percent true, but he would be 100 percent wrong for saying it. So unless he is a complete idiot, the husband will say something like, "Anything you wear looks good to me, but if it will put your mind at ease, then you could always wear something else." He is still telling her the truth, but it isn't more truth than she is ready for. By inviting people to take the next step from where they are, we're giving them the amount of truth they are ready for.

> **Instead of aggressively pushing, we want to lovingly invite. That is why we call it out*reach*, rather than out*push*.**

When Erin met Katie, she didn't push more truth on her than she was ready for. Instead, by showing her God's love and telling her how she was valuable to God, Erin planted a seed. Then I was able to water the seed when she showed up that Sunday. But God made it grow and brought the harvest. That is the essence of kindness evangelism: sowing seeds.

My experience has been that most non-Christians (could we dare to be optimistic and call them pre-Christians?) are somewhere around −6 or −7 on the scale. Most people we encounter have heard about God's love, but they haven't seen it in action. They usually believe there is a higher power, and they are not opposed to the possibility of attending church. *That is why servant evangelism is so effective with connecting with so many people.* When you touch them with a personal expression of God's love, you are inviting them to move to −5 on the scale. For the majority of people who don't yet know Christ, that *is* their next logical step! By meeting their need or doing some act of kindness, you are meeting them right where they are *and* inviting them to take the next step toward God.

When we sow seed in a way that has almost no chance of being effective, we aren't really sowing seed at all. We're littering.

It matters that our approaches to outreach be effective. Some people would say that our outreach efforts should be considered successful based only on the fact that we are obedient because we made an attempt, rather than defining success in terms of the results. I understand the point and partially agree. But when Jesus sent His apostles out to reach other people, He told them to be "as shrewd as serpents" and "discerning" (Matt. 10:16–17).

A discerning farmer sows his seed in soil that is ready to receive it. If he scattered all his seed in a mall parking lot, that wouldn't be very shrewd. He isn't doing anything that is going to produce a harvest. He is just making a mess.

In the same way, if we're scattering seeds in a way that isn't connecting with anyone, then I'm not sure that is really obedience. When we sow seed in a way that has almost no chance of being effective, we aren't really sowing seed at all. We're littering.

By connecting with people through compassionate service, we regularly see amazing things happen. They often ask us to pray about something that is going on in their lives. Sometimes they begin to cry because they had felt hopeless and alone, but now God is breaking through and showing them He is there. They almost always ask questions as they try to reconcile why someone would do something kind for them with no strings attached. They always smile. This is one of the reasons servant evangelism is so fun. It's easy to do something you know is going to make people happy and put a smile on their faces.

Regardless of where a person is on the scale, you can have an eternal impact on his life by fulfilling your role in the process and inviting him to take the next step. Instead of focusing only on the transaction that occurs when a person surrenders his life to Christ, we want to be "*flexible, adaptable, and* able to do and be whatever is needed for all kinds of people so that *in the end* [we] can use every means at [our] disposal to offer them salvation" (1 Cor. 9:22).

Just to be clear, our ultimate goal without a doubt is that a person will respond to the gospel and become a follower of Jesus. The essence of the right response to the gospel is repentance and faith. That is how Jesus invited people to respond to the gospel. "The time has come," he said. "The kingdom of God has come near. Repent and believe the good news!" (Mark 1:15 NIV). The right response now is the same as it was then: repent and believe.

Repentance means I turn away from my sin and my way of doing things and turn toward God. I make Him the CEO of my life. As some people have said, I need for Jesus to take control of the steering wheel. Faith means I recognize that I can never be good enough on my own to deserve salvation. Instead, I trust that what Jesus accomplished through His death and resurrection paid for my sins and made it possible for me to have a right relationship with God. It all boils down to repentance and faith, and when we add anything else as being necessary for salvation, we are in error because we are changing the gospel into something else.

At Friendship we present the gospel every week as clearly as we know how. We are blessed that virtually every week people respond and God radically saves them and changes their lives. We also encourage people to share their faith individually and the story of what Jesus did throughout the week, because salvation doesn't have to happen in a worship service on a Sunday. While we do everything we can to invite people to take *that* step across the line of faith, it isn't the *only* step we present to them. We want them to take the next step toward Jesus from wherever they are, whatever that might be. For some people, the next step might be to stop cussing every time they get angry. For some, the next step could be to forgive someone who hurt them deeply. For some, the next step is to start reading the Bible for themselves. For some, the next step will be to just come back to church one more time as they try to figure out what they believe. And for some, the next step might be to quit their jobs at the strip club because they have just realized how much God loves them. Whatever a person's next step is, we count it as a win when he or she takes it and moves toward Christ. All we did was plant the seed. God made it grow, and we give Him all the glory.

When you meet people where they are, you will connect with them in a relevant way. Since different people are at different places in their spiritual journeys, we do three different types of outreach to cast as wide a net as possible: acts that meet needs (which we call *servant evangelism*), acts of kindness (*kindness evangelism*), and acts of love for our enemies (*Good Samaritan outreach*). There is nothing more relevant to a person than meeting his needs, so that is what the next chapter is all about.

DISCUSSION QUESTIONS

- In I Corinthians 9:19–22, Paul explained how he was all things to all people so he could win as many as possible. How can we find the balance of being culturally relevant to those who don't know Christ, without being overly "consumer focused"?

- Do you agree that there is nothing, short of sinning or compromising the gospel, we shouldn't be willing to do to reach others with God's love?

- What is your next step to meet people where they are? What do you need to keep doing and what might you need to start or stop doing?

- In I Corinthians 14:16–17, Paul reminded the church to be careful not to inadvertently confuse outsiders. What are some examples of how a church might inadvertently create unnecessary barriers that make it more difficult for people to respond to the gospel?

- Is it enough for a church to be doctrinally sound, or should it also be concerned about whether they are connecting with the culture? Why or why not?

- In Philippians 2:3–5, Paul wrote about the importance of being humble and considering the interests of others. Is it hard for you to be humble and consider the other person's interests when the person interrupts you? Or disrespects you? Or maybe when you're stressed? Why?

- In 1 Corinthians 3:6, Paul shows that seeds don't germinate overnight and that only God can make them grow. How can this truth comfort us when we feel that someone we love is never going to change or is just hopeless?

- Are you willing to intentionally defer to someone else today? When someone has a preference that is different from yours, go with hers. If she responds by being shocked because this is so out of character for you, then you'll know you need to do this more often.

SERVE THEM SACRIFICIALLY

When we meet needs, we break down all sorts of barriers.

Not long ago we moved to a new house. Since our "new" house was built thirty years ago, we knew we would have to do some minor work to make it just right for us. When I say "we" would be doing the repairs and upgrades, I am referring to whomever I would hire or nag into coming and doing it for me. I know my strengths and weaknesses, and I know I have no business being involved with any construction project that doesn't involve Legos. But I do have some tech skills, so I put together a beautiful spreadsheet estimating the total cost of the work. Since we had a fairly tight budget, I tallied every expense—moving truck, temporary storage unit, utility deposit, bribe money to get our kids to help, more bribe money to get our kids' friends to help. I thought of everything. When I totaled it all up, I was stoked to realize we still had just enough cushion to be able to also buy our first-ever high-def TV. It was a perfect plan. But I hadn't factored in the cost of new furniture.

I'm a guy. So I had no idea that moving to a new house automatically meant we also had to get new furniture. According to Erin, our old red couch would not be making the trip. Evidently, we now needed a brown couch. Check that—we needed an *oatmeal* couch with *cranberry* pillows. I didn't even know those were colors. My color spectrum doesn't go beyond the eight crayons I had in kindergarten. Besides, sitting on the new oatmeal couch didn't feel any different to my backside than the red one we were leaving behind. But I'm a guy, which means decorating is not in my wheelhouse. So I did what I have learned to do as a good husband and said, "Yes, dear. Let's do what you just said." I keep praying that someday she is going to say those words back to me. Perhaps you could join me in that prayer.

Even though I was trying to be as flexible and gracious as I could, I do have my limits. I reached mine when it came to the new desk. Erin had searched online and found a used desk. We found out it had once been in the office of a particular pizza joint in town, which happens to be something of a landmark in our area. As far as I'm concerned, every pizza restaurant should have

We can design our lives based on appearance and image maintenance or function and purpose.

a monument to recognize the importance of its contributions to society.

Since Erin and I both had great memories of going to this particular eatery as kids, we decided this was the perfect desk for my office. It even had an old menu still taped inside the drawer that listed soda for $0.25. It was very retro and very cool, right up until the moment I tried to sit at the desk. My six-foot, one-half-inch frame literally would not fit. The chair opening of the desk was too short and too narrow for anybody over the age of twelve. And yes, I thought that extra half inch of height was important for you to know about.

Erin wanted to keep the desk. She said it would make a great conversation piece. I didn't understand because that sounded like a really short conversation. ("Did you know this desk was from a pizza restaurant?" "Uh, no." End of conversation.) So we had to make a decision. Were we going to decorate this house primar-ily for looks *or* were we going to design it for function? Since we both agreed I would need a place to work, we ultimately got a different desk that I could actually use. She never did quite admit I was right and she was wrong, but whatever. I'm just glad I finally got my way for once.

At some point, we each have to make that same decision about our lives. On the one hand, we can decorate our lives to be all about appearance and image maintenance. When we do that, most people will probably be impressed, and we might even become a conversation piece. They will look at the way we pres-ent ourselves and assume by our church attendance and the way we talk about God that we must be the real deal on the inside because of what they see on the outside. On the other hand, we can design our lives to be functional. When we choose that route and stop worrying about image, we put ourselves in position to start accomplishing the purpose for which we were created. But before we go all in and begin arranging our lives to be functional, we had better make sure we're crystal clear on what our function is supposed to be. If we're going to reach out to others with God's love, then we have to be about the business of sacrificially serving others.

SMARTEST PERSON IN THE ROOM

Jesus once came upon a guy who was wrestling with the same basic choice that we had to make as we decorated the house: appearance versus function. Would he choose to settle for the mere appearance of being loving, or would he really take the steps necessary to become a loving person? Luke wrote about this guy's conversation with Jesus and how it prompted Jesus to tell one of the most famous stories of all time.

> On one occasion an expert in the law stood up to test Jesus. "Teacher," he asked, "what must I do to inherit eternal life?"
>
> "What is written in the Law?" he replied. "How do you read it?"
>
> He answered: "'Love the Lord your God with all your heart and with all your soul and with all your strength and with all your mind'; and, 'Love your neighbor as yourself.'"
>
> "You have answered correctly," Jesus replied. "Do this and you will live."

But he wanted to justify himself, so he asked Jesus, "And who is my neighbor?" (Luke 10:25–29 NIV)

Luke let us know right away that this guy was really smart, since he was an expert in the law. Luke also pointed out that this man wasn't asking the question from sincere motives. Since the guy stood up and asked this question to Jesus in a very public setting, we start to get a sense of what he was all about. He wanted people to be impressed by him, and perhaps he hoped to prove in front of a crowd that he knew the law even better than Jesus.

The scene reminds me of the movie *Young Guns*. Emilio Estevez plays the part of Billy the Kid. Multiple times in the movie, Billy dares people to try their luck against him in a gun-slinging duel with this simple taunt: "I'll make you famous." Since everyone wanted to go down in history as the person who was an even faster draw than the Kid, they would always reach for their gun. And every time, they would lose because Billy the Kid was the best.

Luke's "expert in the law" was trying to build a public image as someone who was close to God, as evidenced by his extensive knowledge of the Mosaic law. I suspect he thought that winning a debate with Jesus would make him popular in certain circles. He could become the conversation piece that he wanted to be. That is why when Jesus exposed to the listening crowd that the lawyer actually already knew the answer to the question he was asking, the guy was compelled to try to justify himself. He just couldn't

> Knowing God has never been a matter of mere theory and intellect.

let it go. He wanted to be known as the smartest person in the room. But there were two problems with his aspiration. First, he was not going to win the battle, because Jesus, like Billy the Kid, was the best. Jesus' insight into the law was far superior. Second, the guy was mistakenly assuming that superior knowledge of the law was the proof of who was closest to God. But knowing God has never been a matter of mere theory and intellect. Instead, it shows up in the way we love. Jesus was about to uncover both of the errors in a way that made the flaws in this guy's assumptions so obvious that no one could miss them.

I'd rather focus on showing God's love than debating it.

I've always been fascinated by how Jesus handled these sorts of "trick questions." Whenever He knew He was being tested, He wouldn't answer the question directly. He would usually point the challengers back to what they already knew. Often, He did it by pointing them to the Scripture.

As a preacher boy, I get asked a lot of questions, like how to interpret a difficult scripture passage or what the biblical perspective is on some situation. Sometimes it can be difficult to discern whether someone is really looking for an answer or has some other agenda. Whenever the dialogue reaches the point that it becomes obvious he just wants to debate, I point him either to a book someone has written on the subject or to the Bible. Since that was basically the way Jesus handled those types of challenges, I figure it's a pretty good response. Besides, even if I win an argument with him, I'm still probably not going to win his heart. I'd rather focus on showing God's love than debating it. By graciously declining to argue and potentially fracturing my relationship with someone, I can continue to grow my relationship with the person and allow God to continue to pour His love into his life through me.

The guy who was trained in the law asked Jesus a follow-up question: "Who is my neighbor?" Jesus answered, as He often did, with a story. The parable He told not only made clear who was a neighbor, but even more important, it explained how to *be* a neighbor.

> **Jesus:** This fellow was traveling down from Jerusalem to Jericho when some robbers mugged him. They took his clothes, beat him to a pulp, and left him naked and bleeding and in critical condition. By chance, a priest was going down that same road, and when he saw the wounded man, he crossed over to the other side and passed by. Then a Levite *who was on his way to assist in the temple* also came and saw the victim lying there, and he too kept his distance. Then a *despised* Samaritan journeyed by. When he saw the fellow, he felt compassion for him. The Samaritan went over to him, stopped the bleeding, applied some first aid, and put the poor fellow on his donkey. He brought the man to an inn and cared for him through the night.
>
> The next day, the Samaritan took out *some money*—two days' wages to be exact—and paid the innkeeper, saying, "Please take care of this fellow, and if this isn't enough, I'll repay you next time I pass through."
>
> Which of these three proved himself a neighbor to the man who had been mugged by the robbers?

Scholar: The one who showed mercy to him.

Jesus: Well then, go and behave like that Samaritan. (Luke 10:30–37)

This priest was coming from the city where the temple was. For whatever reason, he thought it was best to not get involved. Perhaps he thought it was too dangerous, or maybe he was just in a hurry. We don't know why he didn't stop because Jesus didn't tell us. So evidently it doesn't really matter why.

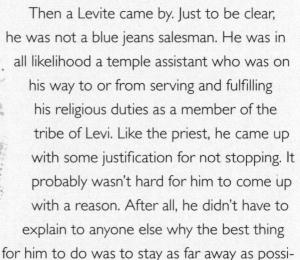

Then a Levite came by. Just to be clear, he was not a blue jeans salesman. He was in all likelihood a temple assistant who was on his way to or from serving and fulfilling his religious duties as a member of the tribe of Levi. Like the priest, he came up with some justification for not stopping. It probably wasn't hard for him to come up with a reason. After all, he didn't have to explain to anyone else why the best thing for him to do was to stay as far away as possible from the injured man and move on. Nobody was watching or judging him for his choice, so the only person he had to convince was himself.

> **Nobody was watching or judging the Levite for his choice, so the only person he had to convince was himself.**

It is interesting, though, that we're specifically told they both kept their distance and crossed over to the other side of the road to pass by. Why did they do that, instead of just continuing on the same side of the road they were already on? It's not like the half-dead guy was going to kick them or anything. Perhaps it's because even though there was no one else around, it was easier for them to ignore the need by looking away and moving away, focusing their attention on a different part of the road, and pretending not to see the need in front of them.

NOBODY IS LOOKING FOR A FRIENDLY CHURCH

One time before I became a pastor and was still a normal and respectable person, I moved into a new area and needed to find a new church. A neighbor told me about his church and said, "You should really come check it out. It's a very friendly church." That sounded much better than an unfriendly church, so I decided to visit. As I arrived on Sunday morning and was waiting to turn in to the church parking lot, another car rear-ended me from behind. The other driver, who was on her way to work, had hit her brakes too late and hit me pretty hard. The collision only dented my rear bumper and axle, but it knocked some parts off of the other car. I know almost nothing about cars or else I would try to impress you at this point by telling you exactly what the parts were. But all I know is they were car parts, so I can only assume the manufacturer had a good reason for putting them on there. We both managed to pull into the church parking lot to try to exchange insurance information and to make sure there was no reason to make a call to Gloria Allred or some other high-powered defense attorney. I'll never forget what happened next.

We hadn't realized that some of the damaged parts that had been knocked off her car were now partially obstructing the church driveway. So since traffic was beginning to back up, one of the church members hopped out of his car, brought the car parts over to us, then hustled inside the building so he wouldn't be late for church. I stood there in absolute bewilderment as one car after another continued to navigate around the broken glass, drive right by the two of us with our obviously damaged vehicles on the edge of their parking lot, and then head on inside the building so they could learn more about how to live like Jesus.

Don't settle for being a friendly person: be a friend.

No one came to check whether we were okay. No one asked if we needed to borrow a phone so we could call for help. No one even offered contact information as a witness to the accident, which would have been awesome since I had finally been in a wreck I didn't cause. As I watched these church people pretend not to notice we were there, I decided this was not the church for me. I had not even set foot inside of the building, but I already knew all I needed to know about the church. I didn't stick around for the sermon that day, but I've always hoped it was about the story of the good Samaritan. That would have been more than ironic.

My neighbor, who had been out of town on that particular weekend, later asked about my experience. When I told him what had happened, he was stunned. "I don't understand! It's *such* a friendly church!" That was when I first realized nobody is looking for a friendly church. They are looking for a friend. There is a world of difference between the two.

When we meet needs, as the good Samaritan did, we break down all sorts of barriers. But when we fail to meet someone's needs, we actually create a barrier that can hinder a person from moving toward God's love, since we chose not to express it when we had an opportunity.

Let's pause for a moment and do some self-evaluation. Are you the kind of friend who notices the needs around you? Nobody's life is perfect. So that means everybody you know has a list of struggles, and there is a number-one struggle at the top of everyone's list. Take out your cell phone right now and look at your call history of the last six people you talked with (or perhaps avoided and sent to voice mail). Do you know the number one struggle each of them is facing?

The sad reality is, we often work and interact with people on a daily basis whose lives are crumbling, but we don't have a clue. We assume that because we're in close proximity to them physically, we would know if they were hurting. Usually we have no idea what they are dealing with because we're not really paying attention or looking for needs to meet. It's as if we have spiritual ADD. Work to be more aware of what the people around you are dealing with and going through. Rather than just asking, "How is it going?" ask follow-up questions so they will know you really want to know. Don't settle for being a friendly person: be a friend.

DON'T MISS THE LAYUP

When I played basketball in middle school, my coach emphasized the importance of scoring the easy points. We spent hours shooting free throws and doing layup drills so we could take full advantage of our opportunities for shots near the basket. Since I was always second-string at best, most of my playing time came either when the starters were tired and needed a break or the score was lopsided and the coach figured I couldn't do much damage. Since I didn't have many chances to score, I always got really excited when I had an easy shot. Sometimes, I got too excited and would overshoot the layup. When I would go into the game and promptly miss a two-foot shot, the coach remembered why he usually kept me on the bench. It's always embarrassing to miss the easy opportunity.

Part of what made Jesus' story so striking when he first told it was that everyone recognized the priest and Levite had regular obligations in the temple. The average person would have seen those two and assumed they were spiritually strong because of their religious roles. The surprising problem with both of them was their worship seemed to end when they left the building where they fulfilled their religious duties. Their obligations at the temple didn't translate into an attitude that affected what they did when they were on the road

Serving others is an essential part of spiritual growth because it breaks the control of self-centeredness in your life.

to Jericho. Their lives were decorated for appearance, rather than function.

Sometimes we do the same thing, but other times I see people make the reverse mistake. Some people love to meet needs during the week, but then they never get involved with serving in a meaningful way at their local church. Make sure your heart for serving others during the week influences what you do at your house of worship. Don't miss the easy opportunity that you have to serve in regular ways with your church.

At Friendship we do everything we can to connect people to regular serving opportunities. Once a person has attended our weekend services about five times, we contact him or her and invite that individual to test-drive some serving role on the weekend, whether as a parking lot attendant or lobby greeter or nursery worker (who we would certainly background check before scheduling to serve with children). If the person tries it and likes it, then we ask him or her to join that ministry team and continue to serve every fifth Sunday, since we have five serving teams scheduled on a rotating basis. On the other hand, if he causes traffic accidents in the parking lot, or she makes babies cry even worse, then we invite that volunteer to test-drive in some other area five weeks later that will hopefully be a better fit. The result is that more than 90 percent of our regular attenders are connected to weekend service opportunities.

It is so important to your spiritual growth that you get plugged into regular opportunities to serve. Occasionally I'll come across someone who basically says, "I just don't think I can commit to serve for thirty minutes every five weeks while I'm at church, even though it requires no extra time out of my schedule." That's okay if people choose to attend and not serve, but I do want them to understand that they are limiting their own spiritual growth and hindering what God is going to be able to do in their lives. They have to make the choice. We ask them to serve, not because we want something *from* them, but because we want something *for* them. We want to see them grow.

Serving others is an essential part of spiritual growth because it breaks the control of self-centeredness in your life. Just as the best cure for being greedy is to start giving stuff away, the surefire solution for selfishness is to begin serving others. As you serve, try to avoid setting limits about what you won't do and when you won't serve. There is a difference between choosing to serve and choosing to be a servant. When I choose to only serve (and it is just one of the many things I do), I keep control over whom I serve and when I serve them and what I am willing to do. But when I choose to be a servant, I give up my rights and my control as I surrender those to Christ. Choosing to occasionally serve when it is convenient makes a statement about my love for my schedule, but choosing to be a servant makes a statement about my love for God.

GET OFF OF YOUR DONKEY

As Jesus told the Samaritan's story, He specifically pointed out that each of the people traveling down the road that day saw this man lying half-dead on the side of the road. So it wasn't as if they didn't notice him. They each recognized they had just stepped into a crime scene. But Sam the Samaritan saw him differently. That probably wasn't his name, but I like assigning names to unknown people in Bible stories because it makes them even more fun to read about. I also usually have background music playing in my head when I read these stories, but we'll talk about that some other time. Sam saw the wounded man in a way that caused him to feel something. Instead of just breezing on by, like the others, he slowed down, got off of his donkey, and did what he could to help. In the same way, we have to slow down, get off of our donkeys (be glad I'm not using the King James translation here), and do what we can to help.

If you are going to be a friend, rather than just someone who attends a friendly church, you have to slow down enough to see the needs that are all around you. I want to make sure you don't miss this, so I need for you to take a deep breath and read the rest of this paragraph with a very slow Southern drawl. You don't need to be more convinced about the importance of serving others. You don't need to resolve to be more compassionate. You don't need another sermon on the good Samaritan. You have to sloooow doooown. Because busyness always trumps kindness. Always.

A few years ago, I took up running for exercise. You may not call what I do running, but I am swinging my arms and moving at an uncomfortable pace, so for me it is running. I built up my endurance and participated in a half marathon. That was definitely a lesson in humility. I started near the back of the pack and still got passed by hundreds of people. I even got passed by one lady who was speed-walking and pushing a stroller. I still don't know why she was in such a hurry.

When I first started running (would you at least let me call it jogging?) in my neighborhood, I started noticing details about my neighbors' homes I had previously completely missed, even though I drove past there at least twice a day. I was suddenly very aware of which families had dogs, and also which ones evidently thought leashes were optional. I also became painfully aware of minor inclines in the road (or as I call them, gauntlets of doom).

One day I went for a walk with one of my kids. That day I saw even more of my familiar street. We noticed which houses had toys in the backyard, which to my child meant perhaps this was a kid who was a potential friend. We saw a turtle at a creek. I hadn't previously even known the storm sewers in our neighborhood fed into a creek. I noticed these extra details about my community because I was going at a slower pace. The more we intentionally slow down, the more details we can see. The faster we go, the more we miss.

There's a big difference between telling people to let you know if they ever need anything as you walk away and stopping to ask what you can do to make the situation better.

When I'm in a hurry, I don't notice the needs around me. When we get caught up in the pace of our culture, other people's struggles become blurs that fade into the background. Even when they are so obvious that we can't miss them, we still don't have time to really do anything about it. So we tell them to let us know if there is anything we can do (and we're banking on the fact they won't), or we tell them we'll be praying for them, or we come up with some other way of removing ourselves from the awkward situation. Then we pass by on the other side of the road and focus our attention on whatever is next on our schedule. There is a big difference between telling people to let you know if they ever need anything as you walk away and stopping to ask what you can do to make the situation better.

It is way too easy for me to invent a reason why I am not the right person to step in and provide assistance. After all, I don't have time to help because I can't be late for work. Or I have to get these groceries home before the refrigerated stuff spoils. Or I need to get home because I forgot to set the DVR to record *Duck Dynasty*. Or I have to get past this broken glass and get the car parked so I won't be late for today's sermon on the good Samaritan. Don't be in such a hurry! Instead, be mature enough to go against your natural inclination, set your own agenda aside, and notice the needs that are all around you.

A FEW DOLLARS AND A FEW MINUTES

Shay was on his way home from work when he noticed a car pulled over on the side of the road. It was the middle of a brutally hot summer day, and he could see someone walking around the car. He didn't usually get involved with situations like this, but he had been learning about servant evangelism at Friendship for the past few weeks. So he slowed down just enough to see if there might be a need for assistance. As he passed by, he saw that the person outside the car was a young lady, and he saw a toddler in the backseat. He said later, "I thought about just going on home, but something about that just didn't sit right with me."

Instead of making sure he got home in time for dinner, he pulled out of the long string of cars going by and pulled in behind her. Since he is not a mechanic, Shay wasn't sure whether he would really be able to do anything beneficial, but he asked the young lady what he could do to help. It turned out the young mom had simply run out of gas. Shay promised he'd be back with fuel in just a few minutes. Since he didn't have a gas can in his truck, he bought one at the gas station and filled it up. He also bought some cold drinks. When he returned with the supplies, the girl insisted that he let her pay him back for everything. But Shay explained he had been looking for a way he could show God's love, with no strings attached. So instead of getting reimbursed, he gave her one of our church's servant evangelism cards and went on his way.

The single mom showed up at church the following Sunday. A couple of weeks later, her brother and his fiancée came too. I found out secondhand that her brother was an atheist, but he just wanted to see what kind of church had helped out his sister on the side of the road. To make a long story short, he and his fiancée have both placed their faith in Christ. I have been privileged to baptize them, officiate their wedding, and watch them begin to raise children of their own in a Christian home. It all started with someone who was willing to be a few minutes late on his way home from work and to invest a few dollars and a few minutes to meet a need that dozens of other people drove right past.

None of us would say we're striving to become more selfish. Most of us would probably also admit we're not nearly as focused on others as we would like to be. If you don't take steps to intentionally shift to an others-centered way of thinking, then your own natural inclination will always cause your focus to drift back toward yourself. You've got to decide to swim upstream and not let your busyness and responsibilities keep you from serving others.

DO WHAT YOU CAN WITH WHAT YOU HAVE

In all likelihood, Sam the Samaritan didn't have an Acme first aid kit packed on his donkey. So where did he get the bandages? He probably ripped up his own clothes and used them to stop the bleeding. Regardless of whether he did that or not, he used what he had to do what he could. He didn't assume someone else would do it. He didn't worry about what was next on his schedule. Where others talked themselves out of getting involved, he talked himself into making a difference.

Almost every week I get an e-mail or phone call from someone thanking Friendship Community Church for serving him or her in some way. I am thrilled that our church has the reputation in our community that we will use what we have to do what we can. We're convinced that if someone is hurting, then the church should be the first on the scene to offer help. But it takes continual effort to keep that core value elevated to its proper place. Occasionally I get a different type of e-mail. It will be from someone within our church who says, "I don't know whether you are aware of the need in this other person's life, but I wanted to let you know so the church could step in and do something about it."

When I get that e-mail (and fortunately, I don't get it much anymore), I reply as graciously as I know how and essentially say,

"I agree this is a need the church should try to meet. Since *you* are the church, let me know what you decide to do about it. I suspect that God put this need in your path and allowed you to see it for a reason."

It is one thing for our church members to see a need. But if they decide someone else should do something about it—even if that someone else is the church—then they're ultimately no different than the priest or the Levite in Jesus' story. We don't want people to simply see a need and feel pity. We want to retrain them to talk themselves into making a difference.

Jesus' half brother James wrote about the importance of taking action.

> Brothers and sisters, it doesn't make any sense to say you have faith and act in a way that denies that faith. *Mere talk never gets you very far, and* a commitment to Jesus only in words will not save you. It would be like seeing a brother or sister without any clothes *out in the cold* and begging for food, and saying, "Shalom, *friend,* you should get inside where it's warm and eat something," but doing nothing about his needs—*leaving him cold and alone on the street.* What good would your words alone do? The same is true with faith. Without actions, *faith is useless. By itself,* it's *as good as* dead. (James 2:14–17)

I'm pretty sure if James were writing this here in the South, he'd say, "When y'all see a need, don't just say, 'Well, bless your heart!' and that you'll pray for them. Y'all step up and be the answer to their prayers."

As you become more aware of the needs around you, you'll find some that you will need to get others involved with to respond adequately. For example, when Katie left her job at the strip club, Erin contacted a human resources director in our church to help get her connected with other employment possibilities. Erin didn't have the right connections to help her find a new job, so she involved someone who did. You'll encounter some issues so large that it will require you to work with a group of people to address them, such as your small group or Sunday school class. But even when you're alone, you can still do what you can with what you have, just like Sam the Samaritan. Being compassionate isn't about having sympathy and hoping the situation will improve. Compassion rolls up its sleeves and does what it can to change things for the better. It certainly takes more time to get involved than it does to send an e-mail asking someone else to get involved. But if we never serve anybody when it's inconvenient, then we'll never serve anybody.

> If we never serve anybody when it's inconvenient, then we'll never serve anybody.

TIME IS ON MY SIDE

Sometimes it seems as though we take a cable-company approach to meeting needs. "I'm sorry to hear about your situation. It looks like I'll be available to show God's love in your area sometime between one and four this afternoon, or else the next available window will be next week. Please press "1" if you'd like to schedule a servant evangelism appointment."

Perhaps you've heard of the study that John Darley and Dan-iel Batson did at Princeton in 1973.[1] They met individually with forty seminary students and did an experiment with three vari-ables. First, the students had already been surveyed to find out whether they had chosen to study theology simply to have a good career or for personal spiritual fulfillment. The researchers told the students that as a follow-up to the survey, they needed the students to give a brief impromptu talk so the researchers could observe their ability to think on their feet. The second variable, though, was actually that some students were asked to speak about whether ministry could be done more effectively from a professional ministry position versus some other career field, while others were given the scripture about the good Samaritan as the source of their talk. The third variable condition was how hurried the students were made. After being given directions on how to get to the building where they would be evaluated, the high-hurry group was told they were already late, the evaluator was waiting on them, and they should hurry. The intermediate-hurry group was simply told the evaluator was ready for them, so they should go right over. The low-hurry group was told the evaluator wouldn't be ready for a few more minutes, but they might as well head on over and may have to wait for a bit after they get there.

On the way to the other building, each student passed through an alley where a man (whom they didn't know was part

The more I embrace an attitude of being fully ready to serve, the more opportunities God gives me to show His love.

of the real experiment) was slumped down in a doorway, with his head down and eyes closed. As the student passed, he would cough twice and groan. Which seminary students would be the good Samaritan to this person in need?

The researchers found that the seminary student's reason for going into ministry had no bearing on his likelihood to stop and check on the man. They also learned that, surprisingly, the students who were preparing to talk about the good Samaritan were no more likely to provide assistance than the others. The only factor that mattered was how much of a hurry the students were in. Sixty-three percent of the low-hurry students offered direct or indirect relief to the man, 45 percent of the intermediate-hurry group provided aid, and only 10 percent of the high-hurry group extended a helping hand. Being in a rush can turn an otherwise compassionate person into someone who is completely indifferent to suffering.

What about your schedule needs to change for your beliefs to be translated into your behavior? Sometimes we need to choose to serve, even though we don't feel like it at the moment. Or when we're tired and would rather take a nap. Or when getting involved would mean throwing our meticulously planned schedule out the window. I realize that if you are as obsessive-compulsive about your schedule as Erin, then you may have temporarily stopped breathing on that last sentence. It's going to be okay. Just take a deep breath and keep reading.

There is no doubt it is hard to stop and meet a need when you have an appointment to be somewhere else. That is why we have to be intentional about it. I'll bet, though, that when you arrive late to a meeting and explain that the reason you are late is that you stopped to help someone and demonstrate God's love, the other parties will not only be understanding—they will be inspired. They'll see you creating a legacy they admire and want to have too.

My experience has been that acts of love don't always have to be big and dramatic to be powerful. When you buy lunch for people you don't even know or offer them a drink or take back their grocery cart, you make yourself available to be used by God to communicate His love. No matter how the recipient of your kindness responds, one guaranteed result is that you will be a bit more Christlike. So figure out a way to stay alert to the needs around you. Perhaps you'll want to set a reminder in your e-mail calendar. Maybe you'll want to do what I do and begin serving someone every day at lunchtime. Do whatever works for you, but do something to make serving others a part of your daily routine.

A while back Erin and I decided we would start setting aside a certain amount of money each week to meet any needs we encountered that week. From the moment we made the decision, it was amazing how each week a significant opportunity would present itself to us. Whether it was a single mom who was struggling to make ends meet, or a health service someone needed and couldn't afford, or someone who was out of work and wondering where God was in their situation, it became obvious to us every single week whom God was wanting us to bless with what we had. What we give may not always be enough to completely change their lives, but it always makes the situation better, and it always encourages people that God has not forgotten about them. Before we give our gift, we always talk the situation over with our three boys. I love involving them in the process because they will grow up seeing acts of kindness as a normal part of what it means to follow Christ, rather than a radical concept that is foreign to them. We often don't share people's names with them, since some of our kids are too young to completely understand the importance of confidentiality. But we always make the decision as a family that this is the situation God wants us to invest in this week. Then we all sign a card that we include with our gift to simply tell the recipients that God loves them, and we do too.

The crazy part is before we made this decision to set aside money each week, I'd go months without being aware of the types of needs we now are meeting on a weekly basis. Perhaps I just didn't notice the needs because I was in too big a hurry. Or maybe God just didn't bother to show them to me because I wasn't going to do anything about them anyway. I just don't know. But I know this: the more I embrace an attitude of being fully ready to serve, the more opportunities God gives me to show His love.

LOOKING FOR AN EXCUSE TO SERVE

The lawyer asked Jesus, "Who is my neighbor?" He wanted to know who he was obligated to serve. That was the wrong question. Through his story, Jesus showed that the right question isn't *who* I should serve, but *how* I should serve. When it comes to loving my neighbor, everyone is my neighbor. When I see a need and my first question is whether this is someone I should help, I am already well on my way to talking myself out of doing anything, because I'm asking the wrong question.

Too often we focus on the wrong question. We see a need and hesitate. When we do that, we lose our sense of urgency. We start thinking someone else will probably do something. Instead of talking ourselves out of getting involved, let's start talking ourselves into making a difference.

Solomon wrote, "Do not withhold what is good from those who deserve it; if it is within your power to give it, do it. Do not send your neighbor away, saying, 'Get back with me tomorrow. I can give it to you then,' when what he needs is already in your hand" (Prov. 3:27–28). If we're going to reach the people in our communities, then we have to be ready to serve others by doing what we can with what we have. When we talk ourselves out of showing kindness to someone, then we're not all that different from the lawyer who asked Jesus how to inherit eternal life. Love becomes a concept to be debated and analyzed, rather than something we do.

A lot of us are what I would call "selectively lazy." We're very busy and are doing lots of things. We just aren't always doing the *right* things. We allow the urgent parts of our lives to crowd out the parts we would say are really more important. Over time, we become fairly comfortable with the discrepancy between our supposed values and our actions because we like that we're getting the urgent things done and checked off of our list. So we choose to stay comfortable, rather than making the effort to do what we would agree is really more important, like helping someone in need. We're busy and lazy at the same time.

Sometimes I'm not just selectively lazy: I'm flat-out lazy. When it is the middle of the night and I hear the dog barking to go outside and relieve himself, my focus isn't always on doing the right thing. Instead, I'm dialed in on what is most convenient. So I elbow my lovely wife so she can deal with the dog. Since she is a sound sleeper, that first elbow never works. So I lovingly whisper in her ear, "I think I hear the dog." She still doesn't flinch. So I say with conviction and quite a bit of volume, "I said, I think I hear the dog." That does the trick. For some reason, when Erin wakes up, she immediately gets on her feet. So as she bolts out of the bed, I bury my face in my pillow, pretend to be asleep, and in a performance worthy of an Oscar, I mumble, "Do you want me to get up and take the dog out?" When I do that (and yes, I really have done that), I've talked myself out of doing the right thing. I've withheld good from someone who deserved it.

A few years ago at Friendship Community Church, we were teaching on this issue of serving others and decided to do a "reverse offering." This is where the church gave everyone in attendance an envelope with ten to twenty dollars. This was "seed money" for them to use to meet the needs they encountered as they went through their week. If they decided to kick in some of their own money to do whatever needed to be done, then that was even better. We had lots of amazing things happen that week, and people came back with all sorts of cool stories.

After we had completed the effort, two things stood out to me. First, no one came back and said, "I couldn't find anybody to help." That told me there were needs all around us in our everyday lives that we normally either hadn't been seeing or just hadn't been doing anything about. My second observation was that nobody in our church seemed to keep showing kindness at the same level after that week had ended. That was because we had inadvertently introduced serving others as something that was special and unique as a one-week emphasis, rather than taking steps toward making it become natural and repeatable. On top of that, we had made it so convenient by giving everyone the money to meet the need, that our people didn't experience any sense of sacrifice as they served. The result was we had an incredible week of serving others—and then everything went "back to normal."

The result was we had an incredible week of serving others—and then everything went "back to normal."

I'm so glad we have changed that within our church culture today. Serving others sacrificially is now part of our DNA and has become the new norm. We still do lots of churchwide serving projects, such as giving away a tractor-trailer of groceries or building a Habitat for Humanity home. In fact, we're intentional about scheduling one of these major initiatives at least every three weeks. But we're now also very intentional about con- stantly pushing the planning and leadership of community minis- try opportunities down to as small a group as possible. Whether it's one of our small groups or a ministry team or some other small gathering of people from within our church, we continue to challenge and encourage smaller groups of people to reach out by serving others.

Here are some examples of how small groups of fewer than twenty people from Friendship have served in our community. Perhaps these will give you some ideas of how you can get started with your small group or Sunday school class.

- **Construction of therapy room:** One group of volunteers helped build an addition to a local family's home as a therapy room for their two children with disabilities.

- **Bridge Ministry:** Another small group partnered with a local nonprofit organization to provide a meal and a worship service, serve as prayer partners, and distribute free groceries and toiletries for the homeless in Nashville.

- **Senior adult assisted-living facility:** Multiple groups have served at various assisted living facilities in a number of ways. One group painted the ladies' fingernails, washed eyeglasses, and distributed goodies. Another group played bingo, served refreshments, and sang to the residents. Still another group worked with children to do a three-stage project: painting flowerpots, putting dirt and plants in the pots, and then delivering the plants to the residents. Children also delivered blankets that had been crocheted by incarcerated women, in conjunction with a prison ministry.

- **Brooks House:** Another small group at Friendship served a local homeless shelter for women and children by painting, cleaning, and organizing a storage facility, and doing minor repairs.

- **Backpacks program:** We provide food packs to send home with local elementary children living in "food insecure" homes. Groups of kids are able to serve other kids by assembling the packs and preparing them for distribution.

- **Local nonprofit facilities:** One group sorted used shoes to prepare for distribution to people in need around the world. Another group sorted food at a major local food bank.

- **Lakeview Elementary:** Multiple groups served at the school where our church met for Sunday worship. One group repainted halls and doors. Another landscaped, cleaned out flower beds, and added pine straw.

- **Trail beautification:** Another small group coordinated a beautification project on a local bike trail by repairing the trail and bike jumps and painting buildings along the trails to clear graffiti.

- **Operation Stand Down:** This group provided office help for a local veterans facility, packed food bags, sorted socks and clothes, assembled hygiene kits, and worked in the thrift store.

- **Women's Hope Center:** A group of women provided, prepared, and served a meal for the amazing women and children at a local homeless center. Hairdressers also gave free haircuts.

- **Master's Hands:** A group of men provided minor repairs and yard cleanup for those who were unable due to their health or age.

- **Refugee Center:** A teen group has served at the center in a number of ways. Some of the teens assisted refugees with preparing for their citizenship tests (including teaching them how to read and write), while others provided child care and activities for their children. They also set up apartments for new refugee families who are just arriving in the country. They distributed items that people donated (anything from food to purses) to ladies at their apartment complexes.

And they conducted a fall festival for the children, with inflatables, a puppet show, food, games, balloon animals, and face painting. Most of the immigrants are Muslim, and they refer to the teens as the "young Christians" and their "good teachers."

> **Rather than saying, "Someone should do something about that," let's ask, "What are *we* going to do about that?"**

- **Christmas gifts:** One of our small groups provided gifts to all the women and children at a local home- less shelter.

- **Lantern Lane Farm:** Our small groups have also served a local counseling center/farm that serves children with tragic family losses. They scrubbed fences, cleared brush, painted, did household chores, and cared for the animals.

- **Oil changes for single parents:** Some of our volunteers pro- vided free oil changes and car washes to single parents (both men and women), while others held indoor activities for their children.

There are all sorts of benefits to empowering small groups to meet needs and to show God's love through acts of kindness, rather than relying only on churchwide projects to reach the community. The group's smaller number of people and lack of resources force them to innovate and be creative. The small group is more entrepreneurial and takes more ownership of the project, since they themselves decide what type of project to do. They are probably doing something they are more naturally passionate about. Since the group is small, there is also more individual accountability and more opportunities for people to both lead and build relationships with others in the group. And perhaps most important, it creates a mind-set within the group that biases them toward action.

When our groups encounter a need, rather than saying, "Someone should do something about that," increasingly the first question they ask is, "What are *we* going to do about that?" Just last week a lady who attends one of our women's small groups fell and broke her ankle. She has no insurance and was now temporarily unable to work, which meant she couldn't afford to get a cast to allow her ankle to heal properly. The ladies in the group all chipped in and together paid the three hundred dollars for her to get the cast. She was speechless at the way her group had stepped up and generously shown God's love. Here's the coolest part of the story to me: by the time the church staff found out about the need, it had already been met. That's what can happen when people are continually on the lookout for how they can serve the people around them.

We saw another example of how this attitude has trickled down during our recent gas buy-down event. We served the community by giving people five dollars in free gas at an area gas station. Our volunteers were given prepaid gift cards to use during the project. When we reconvened at the end of the project, we found out that many of our volunteers had at some point pulled out their own credit cards to give someone a full tank of gas because they sensed a real need. We knew then that serving was increasingly becoming a way of life for people.

Remember *why* Jesus told the good Samaritan story. The lawyer asked who he was supposed to demonstrate love toward. Jesus' answer: anybody you see who has a need. Why? Because loving God and loving others are the most important things you could ever do.

Don't underestimate the power of one act of service. People often talk about how good it feels when they serve others. That's true because it is what you were created to do. You've read lots of ideas in this chapter. Here is my challenge to you: do something to show someone God's love today. Even if it's late at night and you're going to have to get creative, find a way to serve someone right now. Here's why I don't want you to put this off. When you see what a difference one act of service can make, I guarantee you're going to be hooked. You're going to be eager to do it again because showing God's love is contagious.

DISCUSSION QUESTIONS

- Jesus said that what is most important is loving God and loving others. Is it accurate to say that you can see our love for God by the *way* we show our love for others?

- Jesus told the lawyer, "*Do this and you will live*" (Luke 10:28 NIV; emphasis added). Was He saying a person can earn salvation by doing good deeds? In other words, will perfectly obeying the law really get you eternal life?

- Suppose you decided for whatever reason that you did *not* want to be like the good Samaritan. Like the Grinch, you want to be the opposite. If you wanted to become more consistent at *not* seeing people's needs, how would you go about cultivating that habit?

- So what does that tell you about what you need to do to become more like the good Samaritan? How will you develop the habit of more consistently seeing and meeting people's needs?

- In this chapter you were each challenged to find out the number one struggle of the six most recent contacts on your cell phone. Have you gotten started on that? What have you found out about those people?

- Is it possible to see a need *and* feel pity, but still not do anything about it?

- What are some of the reasons we could potentially use to talk ourselves out of helping someone in need? What are some of the ways we could talk ourselves *into* "getting off of our donkeys" and making a difference?

- Most acts of kindness cost us far less than it did the Samaritan. What act of kindness are you going to do this week (or have you already done)?

SOW SEEDS
OF KINDNESS

> We need to
> make sure
> we don't
> confuse
> the method
> with the
> message.

Dick Fosbury liked to play sports. The only problem was he wasn't very good at them. I can relate. I was always just good enough to make the team, but never good enough to start. Dick had one thing I didn't have, though: height. He was six feet, four inches tall by the time he stopped growing. Despite being one of the tallest kids in school, he didn't make the basketball or football team. So he decided if he tried a less popular sport, maybe he would have better success since there would be less competition. That idea led him to the high jump.

Unfortunately, he wasn't so great at it, either. While he was in college, someone bet him he couldn't jump over a stuffed leather chair. He not only lost the bet, but also broke his hand in the attempt.

His coach tried to teach him to do the high jump the same way everyone else did it. Most

113

people used the straddle method, or a variant called the "western roll," where the athlete flings himself over the bar facedown. A few competitors still used the old-school, scissor approach, which meant jumping and swinging one leg and then the other over the bar, before landing on their feet. Dick's personal best with the western roll was 5 feet and 4 inches, which was two feet short of the world record at the time. The obvious conclusion most people would draw was that he just wasn't cut out to be a high jumper. But Dick had one other attribute that would serve him well: he was persistent.

He attempted a new personal best by lifting his hips as he cleared the bar, which caused his shoulders to go back. People said it looked like he was "flopping" over the bar. They laughed because it looked so silly. But it worked. Dick immediately improved his personal best by six inches.

He continued to improve his technique and eventually snagged the very last qualifying spot on the 1968 U.S. Olympic team. The other Olympic athletes didn't take him very seriously. He was considered a novelty, since he had still only risen to a world ranking of 61.

When you've only seen something done one or two basic ways, then anything different will automatically appear strange and you'll view it with suspicion.

When he arrived for the Olympics in Mexico City, he was a complete unknown who had never competed internationally. When he jumped for the first time as an Olympian, the crowd of eighty thousand literally laughed.[1] His technique was so unusual that everyone noticed him. After the first few rounds, his funny motion had made him the crowd favorite, and people began to cheer for him. In fact, the crowd became so engrossed in the high jump competition, they barely noticed when the first marathon runner arrived in the stadium. By the end of the day, Dick Fosbury had made history using the technique that would forever be known as the Fosbury Flop. He won the gold medal and set a new Olympic record for the event as he cleared the bar at 7 feet and 4 inches.

As he launched himself to fame, Dick revolutionized the sport. His technique was adopted so quickly by so many more talented athletes that four years later he wasn't even able to qualify for the Olympics. What I find fascinating is that when you watch footage today of the 1968 Olympic high jump event, everyone else looks weird except Dick. But to the crowd in the stadium that day, Dick was the one whose technique was completely bizarre.

CAN THIS REALLY BE OUTREACH?

The idea that an act of kindness can be an effective evangelism method may seem as outlandish to you today as Dick Fosbury's high jump method seemed in 1968. When you've only seen something done one or two basic ways, then anything different will automatically appear strange and you'll view it with suspicion. There is nothing inherently wrong with traditional evangelism methods. We just need to make sure we don't confuse the method with the message.

If Dick had used the same method as everyone else, he would have limited what he could accomplish. His goal never changed. He was always focused on getting over the bar. What changed was his method. Since the existing techniques didn't mesh with his natural talents and abilities, he designed an approach that capitalized on what he was able to do. He wasn't nearly as interested in doing it the same way as everyone else as he was in accomplishing his goal and maximizing his jump.

The conventional evangelism approaches usually work best for Christians who are naturally extroverted, can relate well with others, and have a decent amount of Bible knowledge. But to a person who doesn't have those qualities, that approach to outreach can seem like setting the high bar at seven and a half feet. It may even seem so impossible to you that you conclude outreach just isn't for you and decide to leave it to those who are elite.

Part of the beauty of doing outreach through acts of kindness is that anyone can do it. You don't have to be an expert. Anybody can pour coffee or pump gas or wash windshields. Even if you're an introvert, you can still be kind to people in ways that don't require a lot of personal interaction. The method changes, but the goal never does. The goal is still to invite people to take the next step toward Christ, and ultimately to reach a point of repentance and faith. It doesn't matter whether you do it the same way as everybody else. What matters is that you capitalize on the abilities and opportunities God has given you and reach out to others. When you do, you can reach people with the message of God's love at a level that perhaps you never thought you could. You can reach people like Gary.

Gary was starting to wonder if there was any point to his life. His wife of fifteen years had left him and the kids so she could pursue a new relationship. Since he was now the sole provider as a single parent, he knew he needed more stable work than the short-term contract jobs he had done in the past. He packed up his family and moved to an area of the country where he had been told work would be easier to find. That seemed like nothing more than a bad rumor now, as he struggled to find a job. He had no friends in the area and was running out of options. As he drove to Wal-Mart one morning, he did something he hadn't done very often. He prayed. He asked God to show up for him somehow in some way if He was real. Gary just wanted to know he wasn't alone.

The method changes, but the goal never does.

As he was leaving the store and getting in his car, he noticed a card on his windshield, stuck under the wiper blade. He thought, "Great—someone else trying to sell something. If they knew how little I had, they wouldn't have bothered." He picked up the card intending to simply throw it away, when a picture of a smiley face caught his attention. He read the card: "We washed your windshield today just to say that God loves you. Let us know if we can be of further assistance."

He scanned the parking lot and saw two guys wearing orange T-shirts, systematically moving from car to car and cleaning car windows. He was headed toward them to say thanks, when a third person wearing the same orange shirt seemed to appear from nowhere. She said, "Could I offer you a free cold drink? Which do you want—Coke, Diet Coke, or water?"

Gary said, "Are you serious? You're just giving these away? You're with the guys over there washing the windshields, right?"

"We're doing it to show God's love in a practical way with no strings attached. When Jesus was here, He served people by washing feet. So we thought we'd serve people by washing windshields," she replied, smiling. "So what kind of drink do you want?"

They talked for a few more minutes, and Gary asked some questions about the church. He left that day knowing God had answered his prayer. He knew he wasn't alone, and somehow that made things seem better. He wasn't sure where this was headed, but he decided he was going to take the kids to church on Sunday to find out more about knowing God and to discover if there was a purpose to the stuff he was going through.

MORE THAN MEETING NEEDS

As we read through the New Testament, there are certain concepts and phrases that begin to stand out because they appear over and over. One of those is the instruction to do good. The directive is phrased a number of different ways: "Be rich in good deeds," "Be kind," "Let your light shine," and "Do good works" (1 Tim. 6:18, Eph. 4:32, Matt. 5:16, Eph. 2:10, NIV). What's interesting is that sometimes doing good deeds involves meeting people's needs, but sometimes it is clearly something else. One of the most profound examples led to a disagreement between Jesus and His own disciples.

> Now when Jesus was in Bethany, at the home of Simon the leper, a woman came to Him with an alabaster vial of very costly perfume, and she poured it on His head as He reclined at the table. But the disciples were indignant when they saw this, and said, "Why this waste? For this perfume might have been sold for a high price and the money given to the poor."
>
> But Jesus, aware of this, said to them, "Why do you bother the woman? For she has done a *good deed* to Me. For you always have the poor with you; but you do not always have Me. For when she poured this perfume on My body, she did it to prepare Me for burial. Truly I say to you, wherever this gospel is preached in the whole world, what this woman has done will also be spoken of in memory of her."
>
> Then one of the twelve, named Judas Iscariot, went to the chief priests (Matt. 26:6–14 NASB; emphasis added).

The disciples recognized this ointment was worth a lot of cash. As they mentally tallied the money they could get if they sold it in the market, they also thought about how many poor people could be helped with the money. Don't overlook that detail: the disciples were focused on *meeting needs*. Even though the woman didn't use the ointment to help anybody, Jesus still described her act of kindness as a *good deed*. While there are lots of lessons we can learn from this passage, my point is simply this: doing good deeds isn't always the same thing as meeting obvious needs.

It is obviously important that we follow Christ by meeting needs. The problem comes when we cross the line into thinking that meeting needs is the *only* thing that is important. If we, like the disciples, reach the point where we start thinking other acts of kindness are a waste of time or resources because they are preventing us from meeting even more needs, then we can know we have crossed that line.

When I take action to help someone deal with a struggle or hurt, I am meeting a need. Kindness is different because it helps someone who may not be dealing with any sort of crisis. Kindness is simply doing something that benefits someone else.

It would seem most of the disciples grasped what Jesus was saying, since they didn't protest. But it appears this may have been the final straw for Judas. He couldn't conceive that acts of kindness were going to lead to Jesus establishing the kind of kingdom Judas was expecting and had hoped to be a part of.

At Friendship we've always tried to keep a balance in our outreach projects between those that meet needs and those that are acts of kindness. If we focused all of our resources and attention on meeting people's felt needs, we'd limit our outreach only to those who were struggling with the specific life issues we set out to meet. But not everyone has pressing needs or major crises. So by also doing acts of kindness, we're able to cast a much wider net that can reach all types of people, whether or not they are currently experiencing significant felt needs.

If we only know how to connect with people dealing with significant issues, then there are many people we will never reach. In fact, many people in today's culture are increasingly comfortable that they can manage just fine without God. We want to demonstrate God's love for them in a meaningful way, and acts of kindness can do just that.

When we washed Gary's windshield, he wouldn't have listed a dirty windshield as one of his top ten biggest problems. In fact, I seriously doubt he would have included it in a list of his top one hundred most pressing issues. Yet we were able to connect with him on a heart level though an act of kindness.

It's not as though Gary's life was per-fect. If he would have been completely honest about his life situation that day, he would have told you he was struggling with his inability to find work, with adjusting to life as a single parent, and with trying to heal a bro-ken heart. In the days ahead, I got to see God work in Gary's life in each of those areas. But we didn't connect with him by planning an outreach project geared toward single dads with similar troubles. We simply planned an act of kindness. Since God is the One who makes seeds grow, we prayed that He would orchestrate divine appointments with the people who needed to know God loved them, as demonstrated through a free windshield cleaning.

> **What we've found over and over is that by doing a simple act of kindness, which may not meet any obvious need, we often end up connecting with people on a much deeper level.**

What we've found over and over is that by doing a simple act of kindness, which may not meet any obvious need, we often end up connecting with people on a more intimate level. Kindness frequently opens the door for us to meet a deeper need. In fact, when we serve people in this way and then ask if there is anything we can pray with them about, they often open up in surprising ways as they share their current struggles.

KINDNESS IN A LAUNDROMAT

Teresa led her small group to do a two-hour kindness outreach last week at a Laundromat. When she arrived with her group, she announced to everyone in the facility they had come to show God's love in a very practical way. She told the customers to put away their money because her team wanted to bless them by paying for the machines and by serving them personally. The Friendship team brought rolls of quarters, laundry detergent, and dryer sheets. Realizing that many of the people there would have kids with them, the team also brought juice boxes, home-made cookies, and some small toys. They served by helping to carry their laundry in from the car, picking up the tab, folding the clothes, playing with the children, and carrying the finished laundry out to the car.

One recipient of their kindness said, "I didn't even have soap today and was just going to wash my clothes in water." Another said, "Dryer sheets? What a treat! I never get to use dryer sheets." One lady asked if she could call her friends to bring their laundry. Another said she usually has to take her clothes home wet because she can't afford to dry them. A mom of preschool-ers said she had been wondering how she was going to do her laundry and keep her kids occupied at the same time. Another mom said a friend of hers had died just that morning, and thanked them for caring for her children. One lady had just finished cancer treatments and was so weak. She said the team were her "angels" and thanked them for helping her.

All of this impact happened in just two hours. They gave everyone business-sized cards that read, "It's free . . . seriously. This is our simple way of saying that God loves you." As they were leaving, the owner of the Laundromat asked if they could come back tomorrow, because they were great for business. They left the extra soap with him so he could give it to future customers who came and didn't have any. He thanked them and told them to come back anytime.

> "When they see you up close, they're ultimately going to see Me."—Jesus

In my community, most people at a Laundromat are facing challenges. Either they aren't currently able to afford a washer and dryer of their own, or their machine has broken down. When someone is facing a struggle, a little kindness goes a long way. Only time will tell how each of these peo-ple's stories will turn out. But Teresa and her group were effective in sowing seeds and inviting people to take the next step as they gave them a personal experience of Christ's love through an act of kindness.

One key element to kindness evangelism is doing it with no strings attached. Recently at Subway I saw a guy leaving who had just finished his lunch. He paused and held the door open for a lady who was coming in. It seemed like a nice gesture, but not for long. After she came through the doorway and didn't acknowl-edge what he had done, he rudely shouted, "Thank you!" His kindness had a string attached. He wanted some gratitude in return for his courtesy. When we attach those sorts of strings to our kindness, we ruin the potential for people to experience God's love through us.

THIS LITTLE LIGHT OF MINE

Once Jesus sat down on a hill and began to teach the crowd that was following Him. He talked about how they could be blessed and the ways they should be different from the world around them: "You are the light of the world. A town built on a hill cannot be hidden. Neither do people light a lamp and put it under a bowl. Instead they put it on its stand, and it gives light to everyone in the house. In the same way, let your light shine before others, that they may see your good deeds and glorify your Father in heaven" (Matt. 5:14–16 NIV).

Jesus presented an object lesson that His listeners would easily understand. "Do people light a lamp and then put it under a bowl?" Everyone there would have immediately said, "Of course not! That would be ridiculous." Today most of us light our houses by flipping a switch. If you're one of the ten people in America who still has a Clapper device from the '90s, then I suppose you could clap on your lights. Regardless, we all still recognize it would be absurd to light a lamp and then keep it under a bowl. But here's the thing: we do it all the time. We call it church.[2]

Jesus said we are the light of the world. We all come together on Sunday. When we're gathered, there are big lights and little lights, and even supersized lights that are trying to shed a few lumens. Some lights have been shining for a long time, and some have just recently been lit. We learn how to be even brighter lights and encourage each other to keep on shining for a long time. We sing awesome songs like "Go Light Your World" and "This Little Light of Mine." All the while, we're gathered together under a bowl.

Every now and then, we lift the lid and look out. We shake our heads in disbelief at how dark the world out there is. We talk about how bad the people out there need light and how we are so grateful that we have it. Then we take our light and go home until we come back the next weekend and do it all again.

I think Jesus would say, "Since you have light and you see a group of people who need light, how about you go over there to where they are? Let them see your light up close and experience you. Because when they see you up close, they're ultimately going to see Me. When they experience you, they're going to experience Me." Jesus made it clear how we shine our lights: we do good deeds. When people see our good deeds, they won't praise us, because it's not about us. They'll praise our Father in heaven and will be drawn toward Him.

Earlier this week I got a text message from one of our Sunday morning greeters. He was at a gas station, filling up his truck, when he noticed a woman at the next pump who never got out of her car. He realized she was digging through her purse, trying to find enough money to buy gas. He went over and told her she could just stay in the car today because he was going to fill up her tank. She rolled down her window and said, "Are you Jesus?" Talk about an opening! This was clearly someone who was ready to receive God's love. She had seen his good deed and was praising his Father in heaven.

CREDIBILITY WITHOUT A BACKGROUND CHECK

One reason acts of kindness are such an effective outreach tool is because they give our message credibility. Even though people may not know anything else about us, they know we have done something selfless for them that is not only unusual, but probably unlike anything they have ever experienced before. We're not simply talking to them about God's love as a foreign concept or a philosophical idea. We're demonstrating it in a very practical way.

James wrote about the importance of demonstrating our faith. He said real faith cannot be separated from good deeds: "What good is it, my brothers and sisters, if someone claims to have faith but has no [good] deeds? Can such faith save them? . . . Faith by itself, if it is not accompanied by action, is dead . . . I will show you my faith by my deeds (James 2:14, 17, 18 NIV).

Christians in America have become very comfortable believing one way and living another. For example, if you took a poll and asked one hundred people whether they believed it is important to eat healthy, the overwhelming majority would quickly agree that we all need lots of green beans and carrot sticks on our plates. Yet do you know what the top food was at the Texas State Fair in 2012? A fried bacon cinnamon roll.[3] If you're trying to maximize the number of fat grams per dollar, then this item is an incredible value. But if you're trying to eat healthy, you might as well get Krispy Kreme doughnut batter injected directly into your bloodstream. It's a fun food to eat, but if you do and still try to say you're eating healthy, then you're kidding yourself.

James made the same point about faith. If you say you have strong faith, but it never shows up in kindness toward others, then you're kidding yourself. The evidence of authentic faith is good deeds that reflect a heart of compassion. We have a word to describe the person who says he or she follows Christ, but whose life doesn't reflect it: hypocrite.

Not long ago I was driving somewhere and had our two youngest boys with me. I gradually realized that the backseat was unusually quiet. Anyone who has spent much time around boys knows the only times they get quiet are when they are asleep or when they're doing something they shouldn't. So I asked, "What are you guys doing back there?"

One of them replied, "We're just sitting back here saying good words." Busted. I didn't know what they were saying to each other back there, but I now knew it was not good words. Yet they had no problem declaring to me that they were living the good life. They must have learned that habit from their mother. Actually, it is way too easy for all of us to say we are living one way, while we're actually living something quite different.

When people see compassion and kindness actually being lived out, rather than only talked about, it carries a tremendous amount of weight. That's why the dancers and employees at the strip club listen to Erin. She is showing them she cares. When she brings a meal or cupcakes or goodie bags, she is giving them something and expecting nothing in return. They take notice of her selflessness because all of the other people who come into the club are the complete opposite. They're focused on getting, not giving. Katie, the former dancer who is now well on her way to becoming a police officer, goes back to the club with Erin to help demonstrate God's love. One of the dancers recently asked Katie, "How much does the church pay you guys to come down here?" She was still struggling to comprehend why anyone would value her enough to serve her without getting compensated in some way. She couldn't help but see the light they were shining, but she's still trying to understand where that kind of love comes from. When people have such a low view of themselves, it often takes repeated acts of kindness for them to start to believe God could actually love them as they are.

When I make my daily purchase at Subway for the person behind me (or sometimes in front of me), that simple gesture gives me instant credibility. It is completely unexpected for the recipient, and he or she is often not sure how to respond. After I say that lunch is my treat today because it's how I like to demonstrate God's love, the recipient will often say something like, "If you had any idea what kind of day I've had so far, you wouldn't believe how much I needed this." By me investing just a few dollars, God is able to use my gift and break through to another person's heart, despite whatever circumstances he or she may be dealing with. Whoever I bless sees my good deed and gives glory to God.

I'll be honest: I still get a little bit nervous every single time. Part of me wants to chicken out and not do it. But I remind myself that what I'm about to do is going to put a smile on someone else's face and give that person a story he or she will probably tell to five other people before the end of the day. I want God to get that glory. I also remember that ultimately it isn't about me at all: it's about giving another individual whom God loves an opportunity to experience that love. If Jesus was willing to die to demonstrate His love for me, then I can deal with a moment of potential awkwardness to demonstrate love toward someone else. So I trust that God has put just the right person in line behind me, and I go for it.

What is cool is how my small gesture gives me credibility not only with the person I'm serving, but also with the Subway employees. Many days they even give me a free cookie. Even if I'm trying to watch what I eat on those days, I have decided this must be God's way of smiling at me and saying, "Go ahead, big boy. Grab you some chocolate chips." The way I figure it, if the cookies are a gift from God, then the calories don't really count. It's just a theory, but I like it.

> **If Jesus was willing to die to demonstrate His love for me, then I can deal with a moment of potential awkwardness to demonstrate love toward someone else.**

You could get started all by yourself and do either of these outreaches. You could take my idea and start paying for the person behind you when you're going through a drive-thru or in line at the cafeteria. You could emulate Erin's idea and take treats to the employees at a retail store or a fire station or a school or just about anywhere you can think of. Just make sure to connect the dots for the people you serve so they know you're showing God's love, rather than a random act of kindness.

There are also lots of ways to do acts of kindness with your small group or Sunday school class too. Here are some examples of what groups at Friendship have done.

Trailer park "block party": We don't have typical city blocks in our suburban area, so some groups have "adopted" specific trailer parks. With the landlord's permission, the group will set up a few inflatables, grill some hot dogs, and do face painting and balloon animals. This project allows for lots of time to talk with people and build relationships.

Christmas parade: The group makes dozens of gallons of hot chocolate and gives it out for free all along our city's Christmas parade route. In addition to a backpack tank dispenser we assembled for this type of outreach, we also strap a five-gallon cooler into a red children's wagon and pull it along. We have cups, lids, and napkins and give people a special Christmas-themed kindness evangelism card.

Reverse trick-or-treat: We've had groups deliver bags of candy and goodies to local retailers, teachers, fire stations, and other local businesses. We

When people have such a low view of themselves, it often takes repeated acts of kindness for them to start to believe God could actually love them as they are.

also do this project at Easter as a reverse egg hunt or any time of the year to thank people for going the extra mile. This is a great project to do with children and their parents.

Movie in the park: The group promoted and provided a free showing of a G-rated movie that had just recently been released on DVD. They also provided free popcorn, snow cones, and drinks.

One-dollar car wash: People in our community see "free" car washes all the time and know immediately it's really a fund-raiser. So to distinguish our event from those, we conduct a one-dollar car wash. The catch is that when the driver pulls into the parking lot, we explain we're not *charging* a dollar. We're actually *giving* her a dollar to thank her for the opportunity to serve in this way. We have cold drinks and chairs available for people while we're cleaning their vehicles. This project doesn't directly impact as large a number as some other outreach efforts, but it allows for lots of time to talk with people who are being served and to build relationships.

Pray at the Pump: This "gas buy-down" event is always a huge hit. We purchase five-dollar gas cards in bulk; then we have yard signs printed up that say "$5 Free Gas" and "No Strings Attached." At the event, we divide people up into different roles. Some stand near the road and hold the signs, while others coordinate the traffic flow at the gas station to direct cars to the next available pump. We have teams of three at each pump. One person talks to the driver to explain what we're doing, gives him a kindness evangelism card, answers questions, and asks if there is anything we can pray with him about. We also have someone to run the gift card and pump the gas, and someone else to wash and squeegee the windshield. This is an outreach where anyone can find a way to serve, since there are some roles requiring lots of interaction with people and others where they don't have to talk to people at all. The hardest part of planning this project is finding a gas station that won't let liability concerns prevent the team from serving at their location.

Fish fry for honored guests: One group set up a fish fry at a local park and invited families with children with special needs for a free lunch. Another group did the same thing for families of teachers, while yet another did the same for the families of city employees and emergency responders.

Refreshments at the park: Groups have provided bottled water and/or popsicles at local baseball fields, soccer fields, and parks. Groups have also set up water stations at local 5K races for charity and provided refreshments at the end of the course.

Candy cane blast: This project was planned entirely by our youth group. They distributed two thousand candy canes at a local outdoor mall, along with a special kindness evangelism card telling the legend of the candy cane. One retailer invited them inside to give the candy canes to all of their employees and customers. The teens even waited in the long Christmas line for patrons who wanted to go back and pick up one more purchase.

IT ALWAYS TAKES TIME

Demonstrating God's love in these types of ways obviously requires you to invest some time. Getting involved with God's plan for the world will always cost you something, whether time or money or status. Don't trick yourself into thinking you're doing acts of kindness just because you never do anything overtly unkind. If we're not careful, we'll convince ourselves we're kind to others, when in reality we are never spending any time with them. We turn love into a way of thinking rather than a way of life. Doing good deeds the way Jesus described always takes time.

Relationships take time too. We've increasingly tried to shape our outreach efforts to maximize the opportunities for our teams to get to know the people they are serving. For example, when we purchased a tractor-trailer full of groceries and distributed them to people in need, we made sure that as people arrived to get food, we immediately matched them up with a pair of volunteers who would be their hosts throughout their time on our campus. The hosts explained what we were doing, helped get their children connected with the kids' activity area we had set up, asked some basic questions about their circumstances, prayed with them, and then helped them get their groceries loaded into their car. We then had those same volunteers follow up with a phone call the next week to the specific people they had served just to check on them and follow up on any prayer requests. For those families who were later recipients of Thanksgiving baskets of groceries, we arranged to have the same set of volunteers deliver their baskets so they would see a familiar face and could continue to build relationships.

It also usually takes some time before we see the fruit from our efforts. But when we do acts of kindness, we're sowing seeds. That's why it is so important that we not give up. Paul encouraged the church in Galatia to keep on doing good deeds. He wrote,

"Let us not become weary in doing good, for at the proper time we will reap a harvest if we do not give up" (Gal. 6:9 NIV).

I usually want the proper time to be right now. That was why I always got frustrated when we learned about Johnny Appleseed at school. I came home with my plastic bag of apple seeds and planted them in the ground. I was hoping to be picking apples from my new trees the very next day. But after you plant an apple seed, there is always a delay before the harvest. Paul said the same principle applies to doing good deeds. The harvest will eventually come, but it is probably going to take some time.

So don't give up! Sow seeds, and then trust God to grow them. If you make a commitment to sow at least one seed each day, can you imagine what God can do with that? Remember that every day you sow a seed, you are one day closer to seeing a harvest of people connecting with God's love. It isn't possible to debate people into loving Jesus, and we can't legislate them into taking a step toward Christ. But when they see God's love demonstrated through someone like you who is the real deal, it is almost irresistible. So let your light shine.

DISCUSSION QUESTIONS

- In Matthew 5:14–16, Jesus is very clear about how we let our light shine: good deeds. Why do we seem to have a natural tendency to drift toward keeping the light in the bowl, rather than shining it outward?

- If our motivation for serving is that we want to make a difference, then when we stop having success or getting praised, we will probably give up. How can we keep our motivation fixed on the fact that we've received God's love, and our purpose in life is to show compassion to others?

- James 2 says that our faith is proved by our actions. But it is easy for us to become comfortable with *believing* one way and *living* another. Our views on eating right and exercising might be a good example. What are some other examples of truths that most of us would agree with, but our lifestyle and choices don't really reflect the fact that we agree with them?

- Have you ever done an act of kindness evangelism? If so, what fears did you have to overcome?

- If you had ten dollars and you wanted to use it in the next twenty-four hours to show God's love in a practical way with no strings attached, what could you do? Try to come up with at least ten different ways you could use the ten dollars to serve others.

- Could you also find ways to serve people "on the cheap," where it costs almost no money? Try to name five ways you could serve people at little to no financial cost.

- What act of kindness are you personally going to do this week (or have you already done)?

DON'T FORGET THIS GROUP

Intentionally do good for the people who are not like you and who may not like you.

After we finish our Sunday morning worship experiences, I generally stay and help our tear-down team get everything packed away and cleaned up. Erin always sends me a text to let me know where to meet her and our kids for lunch. One Sunday afternoon, I arrived at our favorite Mexican restaurant just as I had been instructed. Since this particular establishment has multiple locations, I confirmed the locale so I didn't repeat the Buffalo Wild Wings mistake I mentioned earlier. I walked in and was all set for chips and salsa when Erin said, "Where's Daniel?"

We have three boys, and Daniel is our middle child. Evidently I was supposed to have him with me and had left him at the school where our church meets on Sunday. I hopped in my truck and made the five-minute drive to the school in less than three minutes. Fortunately, when I arrived I saw that a teacher at the school was already looking after him. The teacher is a regular attender at our worship service and had stayed afterward to get some work done in her classroom. I could tell Daniel had been crying, and I felt absolutely horrible about leaving him alone.

As I scooped him up to reassure him, he told me the story of his experience. "Dad, I was walking around the parking lot after you left. I saw a rotten tomato on the ground, and I was thinking maybe I should go ahead and eat it because I didn't know when I would ever get to eat again." Nice. I'd left him alone for no more than ten minutes, but in his mind he had already concluded that he would probably need to survive on his own for days. He was sure that no one in his family would ever even miss him. Since he was already wrestling with middle child syndrome, there was no telling how much psychological damage I had just done. There clearly wasn't a "father of the year" award in my future anytime soon.

On the way back to the restaurant (with Daniel this time), I asked him how he ended up getting left behind. I knew I was in big trouble with Erin for leaving him, so I was grasping for anything I could use as leverage to show it wasn't really my fault I had forgotten a child. Perhaps he had

Even though someone might be important to us, it's remarkably easy to forget about that person sometimes. It is purely a matter of context and focus.

been playing hide-and-seek or was in the bathroom for a long time. If that were the case, I could spin the story so that Daniel wasn't where he should have been or else I would have seen him. Yes, I was willing to throw my child under the bus if it would keep me out of trouble with Erin. Don't judge me.

That wasn't what had happened, though. He said, "Dad, you told me to hold the door for the lady with the baby stroller until she came out. Well, she never came out that door, so I just kept waiting and holding the door because that was what you had said to do." Ouch. So as it turned out, not only could I not blame Daniel for not being where he should have been, but I was completely at fault because he was doing exactly what I had asked him to do and trying to be helpful. I had flat-out forgotten about him. At that moment I realized two things. First, Erin could now win any future argument with me by simply saying, "Well, at least I've never left one of our kids somewhere." Second, I was going to be spending a lot of money at the toy store to try to buy my way back into Daniel's good graces.

DON'T FORGET THE PEOPLE YOU TRY NOT TO THINK ABOUT

Even though someone might be important to us, it's remarkably easy to forget about that person sometimes. It is purely a matter of context and focus. For example, you might see a person at church or at the office regularly, but then when you encounter him in a different setting (like at the movies or in a grocery store), you struggle to remember how you know him. You recognize the face, but the context has changed. Even though he would be instantly recognizable to you if he was in the normal surroundings, you're not used to seeing him in this different setting.

Because I'm their pastor, kids often connect me completely with the context of church. They associate me exclusively with the school building where our church meets on Sunday. Some parents have even told me that when they drive by the school, their kids will say, "That's where Pastor Todd lives." When they see me for the first time at a fast-food place, it blows their minds. They think they must be seeing someone else who looks like me. It had never occurred to them that I ever left the school or ate at a restaurant. They had so completely linked me with the backdrop of church, it's hard for them to process my existence in any other setting.

In addition to forgetting someone because of a change in context, it's also easy to forget some*thing* when your primary focus is on something else. For example, imagine a hypothetical situation where a wife asks her husband to roll the trash cans out to the road for the pickup service. This well-meaning (and dare I say, honorable?) husband goes to the garage with every intention of taking care of this chore. But as he walks into the garage, he notices some bicycles and toys that somebody else left out. Because he is such a conscientious and awesome guy, he takes it upon himself to put those items away. He does it without expecting anyone to thank or applaud him. He is just a good guy doing his best, day in and day out. Unfortunately, the task of cleaning the garage distracted his focus just enough that it caused him to forget to take the trash cans out. I am sure you will agree that this hypothetical husband should be not only forgiven, but rewarded for his ongoing contributions to the family. I'm not saying any of this has ever happened at my house, but it may have. Here's my point: we're not nearly as good at multitasking as we think we are. When our focus shifts to one thing, it often means it has shifted away from something else. That shift makes it possible for us to completely forget about what we're no longer concentrating on.

For several years now I have been focused on showing God's love in two primary ways: acts of meeting needs and acts of kindness. By meeting needs, I have been able to demonstrate God's love to people with insufficient resources or other pressing issues. By engaging in acts of kindness, I've been able to broaden my scope and connect with virtually anyone in my community, whether they had an urgent need or not. I've tried to keep some balance between these two types of outreach. I thought this was a comprehensive approach to reaching out to my community, until God showed me that it wasn't. There was something Jesus had said that I couldn't stop thinking about: "If you're listening, here's My message: Keep loving your enemies no matter what they do. Keep doing good to those who hate you. Keep speaking blessings on those who curse you. Keep praying for those who mistreat you" (Luke 6:27–28).

> **The inescapable conclusion of what Jesus said is that I have to be intentional about finding ways to show God's love to people I don't particularly like.**

The inescapable conclusion of what Jesus said is that I have to be intentional about finding ways to show God's love to people I don't particularly like. Not only am I to be doing good for people in need and for the people I encounter through acts of kindness, but I am supposed to be specifically doing good to my enemies. Perhaps "enemy" seems like too strong a word, and you can't think of anyone you would classify that way, so let's put it this way. Think about the people who are not like you and who may not like you. Whether you would describe them as your enemies or not, they might be predisposed to assume you are their enemy because of who you are and what you believe.

> Not only am I to do good for people in need, but I am supposed to be specifically doing good to my enemies.

Who is that for you? What type of person is least likely to be in your circle of friends? I'm hoping that in addition to broad categories of people, you can identify some specific names of people you know. So let's rephrase the question: Who is the person that, if you saw her from a distance at the grocery store, you would pretend not to see her and try to walk away before she saw you? Who is the person that, if his name appeared on your phone, you would send the call to voice mail? Who is the person you unfriended or blocked on Facebook? Okay, now we're getting somewhere.

I've definitely thought of specific people, and I'm not going to name them here for obvious reasons. But as I've begun taking steps to live out what Jesus said about loving everyone, God has put two specific groups of people on my heart: homosexuals and Muslims. The only thing these two groups have in common is that they have almost nothing in common with me. I don't harbor any dislike for either of them. We're just completely dissimilar. For that reason, culture says we are supposed to be enemies.[1] Fortunately, we don't have to be. We can choose to show love for the very people who would expect us to be against them.

I've never intentionally excluded anyone as I've expressed God's love. In fact, I have friends who are Muslims and friends who are gay. I have had a mind-set, though, where I tended to focus on reaching out to people who were most similar to me. I knew these other groups of people existed, but it was as if I had forgotten about them when it came to outreach. Similar to when I didn't recognize people in a different setting or forgot to do a chore, it was again a matter of context and focus. I had never specifically thought about them within the context of my efforts to connect people with God's love. Instead, my focus was on who I envisioned as the "average Joe" in my community. The result was I was rarely doing anything that was likely to reach the people who were very different from me.

I'll be honest. I'm only at the beginning of my journey of reaching out to these groups. I've always welcomed them and have worked hard to create an environment in our church where they could safely explore a relationship with God. If they happened to find me, then I accepted them and was happy to be their friend. I've realized that is not enough, though. I have recognized that welcoming someone is not the same thing as actively going to find that individual. My son Daniel has always been welcome in our family. But the day I realized I had left him behind at the school, it wasn't enough for him to know he was accepted and welcome in my home. He needed for me to come and find him. In the same way, I'm now taking steps to actively connect with these people who are different from me.

Jesus said we're supposed to be like the shepherd who leaves the ninety-nine sheep behind to go and find the one that is lost (Luke 15). Sometimes that means stepping out of our comfort zone so we can connect with someone who runs in a completely different circle than we do. That is what Erin did when she made her first trip to the strip club.

At Friendship we've added a third category of servant evangelism project. We've always done ministry projects and acts of kindness, but now we also regularly schedule what we call "Good Samaritan" projects. When we discussed that story earlier, there was one important detail we didn't talk about. Samaritans and Jews didn't interact socially. The Samaritans were a race of people who had intermarried with Syrians, so Jews viewed them as impure. For their part, Samaritans set up their own worship center at Mount Gerizim. They accepted the first five books of what we call the Old Testament, but they rejected all of the Jewish prophets. Neither group wanted anything to do with the other. So when Sam the Samaritan helped the injured man on the road

My primary focus isn't to prove other people wrong with my words, but to prove that Jesus is love with my actions.

that day, he was overcoming some significant cultural, social, and religious barriers.

We need to reach out across those barriers too. Similar to the way Erin began in the strip club, I've begun to intentionally reach out with acts of kindness at events where I know I'll encounter Muslims and people from the gay and lesbian community. I'm not there to pick a fight. If I tried to do outreach by choosing to start a conversation with the point of our most likely disagreement, then that is what would happen. But by demonstrating kindness in practical ways, I'm able to both begin new relationships and allow people to experience a tangible expression of Christ's love through me. When people ask me questions about what I believe or what the Bible says, I answer with grace and truth. My primary focus, though, isn't to prove other people wrong with my words, but to prove that Jesus is love with my actions.

Jesus said, "Listen, what's the big deal if you love people who already love you? Even scoundrels do that much!" (Luke 6:32). As followers of Christ, we need to love people when they least expect it and perhaps feel they least deserve it. When people receive grace from someone they would expect to be the last to show it, they take notice and are forced to respond.

As I mentioned earlier, when you reach out to these people with love rather than judgment, you are going to be misunderstood and criticized. The sad part is it won't be the people you're trying to reach who will bash you. Instead, you'll be denounced by other Christians. They will insist that you should always make sure people know exactly how they are sinning, but telling people all the ways they are wrong is a terrible place to begin a conversation. When you reach out to people they find unacceptable, they will say things like, "We're called to *love* people like that, but we don't have to *like* them." That's a nice sound bite, but it doesn't really make any sense. It doesn't even remotely resemble what Jesus did.

Jesus never began a conversation with outsiders by condemning them.[2] The only interactions He ever began with disapproval were those He had with the religious insiders. When dealing with outsiders, He would eventually challenge them to "pick up [their] cross[es]" and "deny" themselves, and "leave [their] life of sin" (Matt. 16:24 The Voice; John 8:11 NIV). But He didn't start the conversation there.

We often want our enemies' next step to be repentance because we want them to admit what they did to hurt us or how they are wrong. But there may be other steps they need to take first. Jesus accepted the people who were unacceptable and made it clear He wants us to do that too. Not many people ever get condemned into life change. But people get loved into life change all the time. It is God's kindness that leads us to repentance (Rom. 2:4), and He empowers us to extend that same kindness to others.

So don't be discouraged and don't stop. Remember that Jesus was misjudged by religious people throughout His ministry. He was called a drunk, a liar, and a blasphemer. He was accused of being a supporter of Rome and a rebel against Rome. His "super-spiritual" enemies said He deceived people and that His birth was illegitimate. So if religious people treated Jesus with disdain, count it as a badge of honor if they treat you the same way.

We don't love people because they deserve it. We love because He first loved us.

THERE IS NO ONE MORE QUALIFIED TO REACH YOUR ENEMY THAN YOU

Besides reaching out to people with whom we have nothing in common, we're also supposed to demonstrate love toward people who have personally wronged us. I know, I know. You don't have any enemies because you are so awesome. So let's just speculate about how you could reach out to someone who hypothetically unfriended you on Facebook. Let's consider how you could show God's love for someone who is rude to you or annoys you or talks about you behind your back or treats you unfairly or lied to you or seems to like it when things don't go well for you.

Just in case you're still having trouble thinking of someone specific, let's speculate that it could be someone you dated or your ex-spouse. Perhaps your enemy might be the person who "stole" your ex-spouse. Maybe it's a business competitor who got the deal you didn't, or someone who got pregnant when you couldn't. Possibly your enemy could be the president of your homeowner's association or a family member who fell off the wagon again. I'm going to assume you have at least one name in your mind whom you could accurately describe as your enemy.

Jesus said that this person who you may be completely justified in viewing as an enemy is the very person you're supposed to love. Unfortunately, we can't just stay in the theoretical realm and convince ourselves that deep down we really do love the person on the inside, even though it never shows outwardly. Jesus said we need to be intentional about doing good things for him, blessing him, and praying for him. We think, *Sure, I'll pray for him . . . to get hemorrhoids and shingles! Then I'll pray God will heal him . . . in a few years.* That's not quite what Jesus had in mind.

I have to find ways to act in *their* best interest. That's Jesus' definition of how I love my enemy.

For some of us, our natural response to our adversary is to form a posse. We'll talk to other people about how hard the person is to like. We may even be super-spiritual and disguise it as a prayer request. We're not really trying to gossip. We just want to find out if our friends have noticed all of those annoying traits and reached the same conclusion that this person is, in fact, a loser. Since that's our normal way of doing things, we consider it a win when we are able to restrain ourselves and keep our critical comments to ourselves. It isn't.

Others of us would never dream of telling other people how we feel about the person. Instead, we like to fly solo and give her the cold shoulder. We'll play little passive-aggressive games where we don't speak. Perhaps we'll pretend not to see her when she's around or to hear her when she speaks. We might stop calling or e-mailing as often as we did in the past. Since that's our normal way of doing things, we may even tell ourselves that choosing not to lash out or retaliate is the same thing as doing good and bless-ing her. It isn't.

So what does it mean to bless my enemy? Here in the South, there are a couple of normal times when we'll bless someone. The first instance is whenever someone sneezes. We'll reply, "Bless you." If we hear you say, "Gesundheit," we'll assume you speak German. The second instance is whenever someone does something really stupid. We smile and shake our heads and say, "Well, bless your heart." It sounds sweet and considerate, but every Southerner knows what we really mean is, "You are a total moron." Neither of those is the kind of blessing Jesus was talking about.

To bless people literally means to want God's favor on them. That is not quite the same as wanting them to have hemorrhoids. Instead, we are sincerely wishing them well and wanting them to have joy in their lives. As a follower of Jesus, I can make the choice to tolerate my enemies, to refuse to retaliate against them, and can even restrain myself from gossiping about them, but that still isn't enough. I have to do good to them. I have to find ways to act in *their* best interest. That's Jesus' definition of how I love my enemy.

Here is the paradox: you have the potential to demonstrate God's love toward your enemy more effectively than you can toward anyone else.

He says we're to pray for them. When you begin to genuinely pray for someone who has mistreated you, your prayers may or may not affect the other person, but I guarantee they will impact you. You can't pray for someone for very long without God changing your heart. After a while, you'll start to notice little changes in your attitude toward your enemies. When you see them, you won't have the same feelings you used to have. You'll stop feeling the need to change them or point out their mistakes. You may even begin to have a new appreciation for them because you're no longer focused on how they're not meeting *your* needs. Instead, you're focusing on *their* needs, and over time it starts becoming more and more natural for you.

Honestly, there's probably nothing more difficult to do than this. It's not normal to treat someone with kindness whom we've always viewed as a foe or a rival. I've never heard of Republicans having doughnuts and coffee delivered to the Democratic head-quarters, or vice versa. If they did, then probably everyone would be afraid to touch any of it because they would assume it's been contaminated somehow. It isn't natural to do something to bene-fit someone who has wronged us or doesn't like us. *That is what makes it so powerful.* It's not natural: it's supernatural.

On the other hand, as difficult as this may seem to be, for the Christian nothing could be more natural. God loves the person who hurt you the most just as much as He loves you. As a Christ-follower, when you think about your enemy and ask yourself, "What is the most loving thing to do?" your next step becomes obvious. You need to take action to make his or her life better.

When a person intentionally sacrifices time and resources to help someone else, people always notice. When someone does this for an enemy, people are absolutely shocked. They want to know why anyone would do this, because it is so countercultural. They even tell other people about it. Here is the paradox: you have the potential to demonstrate God's love toward your enemy more effectively than you can toward anyone else. Only God's love would compel a person to do something like that for his enemy, so you are the perfect candidate for the job.

BE A TERRIBLE ENEMY

It almost seems there is a universal law dictating that every elementary school must have at least one cafeteria lady who doesn't like kids. My kids' former school was no exception. This lady was the type of person who never smiled. When she was happy, she just scowled less. One time I was eating lunch and playing "I Spy" with the first graders. One of them said, "I spy with my little eye something that is mean." I only needed one guess to win that round. I made a new rule that we could only "I spy" inanimate objects before someone ended up with hurt feelings. Plus I was a little nervous about what they would say if they decided to "I spy" me.

Do you know anybody like that cafeteria lady? Perhaps you're familiar with someone who seems to be in a perpetual bad mood or who is never satisfied with the service in any restaurant. I decided to make a change and start doing nice things for the cafeteria lady. The only way this woman was going to change was if God got hold of her. At first, I brought her sweets whenever I came for lunch. Then I found out she was diabetic and wondered if I was trying to kill her. Strike one. So I had to get creative and went back to the drawing board. I got the kids involved with finding ways to brighten her day too. We did lots of little things to show her kindness and God's love. When our family moved away and we left that school, she was still fairly mean. But I was different. I had learned I could choose to treat someone with kindness even when I didn't feel like it.

It's okay to not always feel like loving. When I ask my kids to clean up their rooms or help with yard work, 90 percent of the time they don't feel like helping. That is why I'm asking them to do it. If they felt like it, they would have already been doing it. I don't necessarily expect them to like it. In fact, if they got fired up and started cheering when I asked them to clean their rooms, that would be weird. I would start to worry I had gone through a wormhole and landed in an alternate universe. I simply want them to choose to obey, even when I know they don't really feel like it.

Similarly, if I waited until I felt like obeying what Jesus said before I did it, I wouldn't obey very often. By definition, when I am not obeying, I am disobeying. So when I'm not choosing to love my enemy, I am disobeying God. But as I choose to obey, over time my heart begins to follow my actions. I'm taking another step that changes me to become a little bit more like Christ. In fact, we will never look as much like Jesus as when we are demonstrating love for our enemies.

YOUR GREATEST OPPORTUNITY TO CHANGE THE WORLD

Everyone has heard of Mother Teresa, and most people would agree she made a huge impact through serving others, but you may not have heard the backstory.[3] Shortly after she had begun her work in Calcutta, ministering to the poor and destitute, she saw a man lying in the street. She saw him move slightly and knew he was alive. Just as in the story that Jesus told of the good

Samaritan, people walked right past him without giving him a second glance. She hurried to help him, but he died right there on the street. This drove her to set up a "Home for the Dying" in an abandoned hostel, which was given to her by city officials. It was a place where dying indigents could come for free to receive medical attention and die with dignity. This new ministry was in the middle of a Hindu region and located right next to a Hindu temple. The Hindu priests continually opposed her work and went to the local authorities to try to force her to leave.[4] They organized protests and made death threats.[5]

One of the local Hindu priests who had led the opposition against her contracted a fatal strain of tuberculosis. The local city hospital had denied him a bed, since it was overcrowded and his illness was untreatable. His own relatives had abandoned him. So Mother Teresa brought him into the home and personally took care of him until he died. After his death, she and the other missionaries carried his body back to the Hindu temple so his last rites could be conducted according to the Hindu customs.

With that act of kindness, the opposition from the Hindu priests stopped. They finally understood that she didn't love people simply because they converted to her religion. She loved them because God loved her, and she demonstrated it through selfless acts of compassion. As a result, the entire city opened up to her, and the repercussions were felt around the world. Mother Teresa made a difference because she loved her enemies just as Jesus did.

What kind of difference could you make? There is only one way to find out. We've got to make Jesus' way our way. So what act of kindness will you do to get started with loving your enemy?

Who do you need to call or write? Whose desk are you going to stop by this week?

Whether you recognize that you have an enemy or not, I guarantee there will be someone in the next seven days who is going to make you angry. What you do when that happens could be the most significant thing you do this week as a Christian. When someone is rude or manipulative or opposes you in any way, a window of opportunity opens for you to reflect God's love to the people around you. So plan to seize the moment and look forward to the opportunity.

One word of warning: don't use this as a weapon. Don't go to your boss and say, "I've been reading about the importance of being kind to my enemies, so I made you cookies. I hope you enjoy them, loser." That's how you make an enemy. Instead, transform an entire situation with extravagant love. When you see someone being rude to a server, pay for his meal and be exceptionally nice to him. Your simple act of kindness will not only radically alter the environment, but it just might inspire the rude person to be different. You can help people see that the path to a better life is through experiencing Jesus' love and forgiveness.

If it is just too difficult for you to love your enemy, there is one other option. You can choose to not do any of this and let your enemy continue to be your enemy. The tension and hostility will continue to escalate. You'll get angry when you think about that person, and the relationship will continue to deteriorate. That is the only other option.

So choose obedience. Loving your enemies opens the doors to God's greatest blessings and the abundant life He promised.

The more a person doesn't deserve your act of kindness, the bigger your opportunity is to show God's love. When a person receives this kind of disproportionate love from a source he or she would have never expected, God can break through to the hardest of hearts. So take the next step, because you will never look more like Jesus than when you love your enemy.

DISCUSSION QUESTIONS

- Jesus said in Luke 6:27–28 to love our enemies. Who are some people that you might instinctively hesitate to accept—whether because of what they're struggling with, or what they do for a living, or what they believe about God? Who might you not naturally accept?

- Do you feel comfortable around people who have low moral standards and who would generally be categorized as "sinners"? Do those people feel comfortable around you? And is that a good thing or a bad thing?

- Since God accepted us when we weren't up to *His* standards, why is it often still so difficult to accept people when they don't meet *our* standards?

- Think back to the people you identified in the first question as tough for you to accept. What if you intentionally showed them acceptance (which isn't the same as approving of all they might do)? What would you do first to show acceptance to those people? What specific steps would you take to get started?

- There is only one way that anyone experiences God's love and compassion: through followers of Christ. What is one practical step you can take this week to allow God's love to flow through you and to others more than it did last week?

GIVE GENEROUSLY

Generosity is an essential trait for anyone who wants to show God's love day in and day out.

Sometimes people ask, "How can you afford to do so much outreach?" Whether they are referring to the money we allocate as a church or that Erin and I invest as individuals, my answer is the same. Reaching others is one of our core purposes, so why wouldn't we designate as much money as possible to that end? Besides, if we don't use it to reach people, we'll inevitably just waste it on ourselves. Generosity is an essential trait for anyone who wants to show God's love day in and day out.

At Friendship we have a policy that we never do fund-raisers. We want to always be a blessing to our community, rather than asking our community to bless us. At the same time, we try to say yes to any donations of items and supplies that we can pass along to others. We've accepted everything from cases of sports memorabilia bobbleheads to truckloads of bologna. Whatever the item, we will find a way to give it to someone as a means of communicating God's love. By being known to local businesses and distributors as a place where they can always unload excess inventory, we are able to build bridges to future opportunities when they need to unload something else so that we can be a channel for generosity.

The goodie bags that Erin delivers to the dancers are almost always filled with items that people have selflessly given. Without the generosity of a number of people, Nashville Strip Church couldn't provide girls a meaningful path forward. When a girl decides she wants to leave the club, prompt job placement is essential. Despite the money most dancers make, their lifestyle is such that they haven't built up any savings. In most cases, it was the need for money that drove them to work at the club in the first place. Then, in an effort to cope with the realities of what they are doing, many turn to alcohol or drugs. They want to numb their minds to how they are devaluing their body. So when a girl takes a step of faith and walks away from the club, she immediately faces a financial crisis. We have a human resources executive who generously donates her time to help the girls put together their résumés, prepare for interviews, and manage their finances more wisely. Other

The bottom line is, being known for love will affect your bottom line.

people donate gift cards and funds to ensure the girls are able to successfully make the transition through the interim period without an income and to the first paycheck of their new jobs.

There are certainly ways you could meet needs and do acts of kindness without it costing very much. You can also free up money by doing something like bringing your lunch from home two days per week to have money to pay for someone's lunch on two other days. But the bottom line is, being known for love will affect your bottom line. It usually takes money to provide food for a hungry person or a winter coat for an underprivileged kid. I wish it didn't, but it does. You don't necessarily have to pay for someone's lunch every day or buy a catered meal for twenty-five people at a strip club to demonstrate God's love. But if you're going to reach out effectively to others, you have to continually become more generous and less greedy.

EN GARDE

I have never been to a fencing match, but I love to watch movies. I've seen *The Princess Bride* and *The Three Musketeers*, so there is at least one thing I have learned about fencing. At the beginning of each duel, someone always says, *En garde*. It is a French phrase that simply means to be "on your guard." If you don't get ready and take a defensive position, you are moments away from being waylaid by a foil.

Jesus warned about how we need to be on our guard too. He was in the middle of teaching a lesson to His disciples and the crowd that had gathered, when a family squabble interrupted everything. Rather than allowing the scene to become a *Jerry Springer* segment, He leveraged it as a teachable moment.

A person in the crowd got Jesus' attention.

Person in the Crowd: Teacher, intervene and tell my brother to share the family inheritance with me.

Jesus: Since when am I your judge or arbitrator?

Then He used that opportunity to speak to the crowd.

Jesus: You'd better be on your guard against any type of greed, for a person's life is not about having a lot of possessions.

(then, beginning another parable) A wealthy man owned some land that produced a huge harvest. He often thought to himself, "I have a problem here. I don't have anywhere to store all my crops. What should I do? I know! I'll tear down my small barns and build even bigger ones, and then I'll have plenty of storage space for my grain and all my other goods. Then I'll be able to say to myself, 'I have it made! I can relax and take it easy for years! So I'll just sit back, eat, drink, and have a good time!'"

Then God interrupted the man's conversation with himself. "Excuse Me, Mr. Brilliant, but your time has come. Tonight you will die. Now who will enjoy everything you've earned and saved?"

This is how it will be for people who accumulate huge assets for themselves but have no assets in relation to God. (Luke 12:13–21)

Jesus could have stopped His story after the very first sentence. He had already made His point. "A wealthy man owned

some land that produced a huge harvest." The man didn't produce the harvest. The ground did. Who made the ground? Who
caused the rain and sunshine? Who caused the ground to produce? Exactly. Whether this rich farmer recognized it or not, he
was ultimately dependent on God. So are we.

In a sense, this story is taking apart the American dream. Isn't
the goal for most of us to reach a point when we, like the wealthy
landowner, can kick back and just take it easy?

Jesus says if our goal is simply to build bigger barns, then we're
fools. The problem would not be that our barns are too big.
There is no passage in the Bible that specifies the
maximum square footage of barns. Jesus is not
anti-wealth or anti-barn. Big barns are good.
I wish I had a bigger barn. But that isn't the
point Jesus is building toward.

Evidently the guy who interrupted
Jesus' sermon didn't recognize his own
greed. Nobody thinks they are greedy.
When it comes to this issue, it is as if we
become vampires: we can't see ourselves
in the mirror. I have never once heard
anybody say, "Please pray for me because
I'm so greedy." *Greed* is such an ugly word that
nobody wants to wear the label. Instead, we describe ourselves
as being thrifty or careful or good planners. So let's get a working
definition of the term so we are on the same page.

Greed is the assumption that everything you have is for you.
Being greedy does not mean you don't believe in God or love

> The irony, for
> the wealthy man
> and for us, is
> that if we live to
> get as much as
> possible, we are
> guaranteed to end
> up with nothing.

people or do lots of good things with your money. It simply means when you are making a big decision, the question you ask first is: "Am I going to be able to get what I want?"

There are only two ways to have certainty about getting what you want. You can either buy what you want right away, or you can save enough to ensure you will be able to buy whatever you want later. Unfortunately, both of those paths to certainty are also paths to greed.

Someone sent me an e-mail recently asking for counsel. She said a pastor in her area had a really big house, and she wasn't sure how to feel about it. She wrote, "I want a black-and-white answer."

So I gave her a very black-and-white response. I said she was fixating on the wrong thing. Generosity leads us to focus on how much we ourselves are giving, rather than how much someone else is keeping. She said she found my answer very frustrating. At least it was black-and-white!

Jesus ended His story with a telling question: "When you die, who is going to get all of your stuff?" The answer for the wealthy farmer is the same as it is for you: somebody else. At some point, everything you own is going to end up at the landfill. It may happen soon, or it may not be for several more generations, but it all becomes somebody else's trash eventually.

The rich guy's error was thinking *his* barn full of stuff was all for *him*. The irony, for him and for us, is that if we live to get as much as possible, we are guaranteed to end up with nothing. When we die, we don't get to take any of it with us. The way we ultimately gain more is by giving more.

RECOGNIZING A GOOD INVESTMENT

My dad grew up on a farm. He told me about a neighbor they had named Vincent. Vincent lived in a farmhouse with his sister, and he gave new meaning to the word *frugal*. Like my dad's family, he didn't have a lot, but he had enough to get by. Vincent just couldn't ever bring himself to spend anything. He held on to every dollar as tightly as he could.

When his clothes began to wear out, he patched them so he wouldn't have to spend money on new clothes. When the patches wore out, he patched the patches. Unlike the other farmers, he never wanted to pay anyone to help him, so he always worked alone. When he brought bales of hay to his barn, he tossed two bales up to the loft. Because the loft opening could only fit two bales at a time, he would then climb up the ladder to move the bales himself, since no one was up there to catch and stack them. His thriftiness meant his work took a lot longer, because he was doing two-man jobs all by himself. It was also a lonely way to go through life.

One time my grandfather had finished up his work, so he took my dad and his teenage brothers over to Vincent's house to help him out. After they had been working a couple of hours and gotten more done than he could do in a week by himself, Vincent's sister pulled him aside. My dad and his family could hear her saying, "We can't afford to pay them! Tell them to go home!"

When Vincent reappeared, he said, "Boys, I appreciate all the help. There's not much left to do, so I'll just take it from here. How much do I owe you?"

My grandfather said, "It's no problem. We're just trying to be good neighbors. You don't owe us a thing."

Vincent said, "Well, you know, I guess I could use some help for a couple of more hours if you've got the time." Once he knew the labor was free, he decided having some extra help wasn't so bad.

That was evidently typical of Vincent. He was so cheap that he didn't even like spending money on seed. When he planted his garden, he would sow the seed so sparingly that there would be bare patches all over his garden where he didn't sow any seed at all.

As Paul wrote to the Corinthian church, he reminded them of an important principle. He said, "I will say this *to encourage your generosity*: the one who plants little harvests little, and the one who plants plenty harvests plenty" (2 Cor. 9:6).

For a farmer, buying seed can seem like a risky venture. It could take a month's worth of income or more to buy enough seed and fertilizer, especially since there are no guarantees of a crop. But if he doesn't take the

**We don't give to get.
We get to give.**

VOLUNTEER

DONATIONS

risk and use the seed for what it is intended, then he ensures two things will happen. First, he won't have to experience the fear that comes with taking the risk. Second, he has guaranteed he won't have any crop at the harvest. By skimping on seed, Vincent mini-mized his risk, but he also minimized his crop.

I don't think it's a coincidence that Paul described his teaching of the gospel as a *seed* he had planted (1 Cor. 3:6), then described doing good deeds as *planting seeds* that would lead to a harvest (Gal. 6:9), and in 2 Corinthians 9:6 describes generosity with the same analogy of *sowing seeds*. Inviting people to take the next step toward Christ, showing God's love through acts of kindness and meeting needs, and being generous are all interconnected. They are each different facets of the process of outreach.

Paul compared our money to seed. Just like the farmer, we have a spiritual crop to produce. But just like the farmer, we also have only a limited supply of seed. Paul says the wisest move we can make with our money is to sow it.[1] When we do give, we will reap a harvest. God gets involved in our lives, and His blessings cannot be stopped. But we have to first give it away in faith.

While God promises blessings, you may not see the return on your investment in this lifetime. But you often will as God blesses you emotionally, relationally, spiritually, and sometimes even finan-cially. Some people teach a "prosperity gospel" that says when we give money away, we are guaranteed the money will always come back to us, and perhaps even be multiplied. In other words, they teach that we should give more in order to get more. But if that is our motive for giving, then whom are we really worshipping: God or money? We don't give to get. We get to give.

Jesus famously said, "It is more blessed to give than to receive" (Acts 20:35). He didn't say those words just to give us a nice quote to put on our Christmas cards. He really meant it. Jesus knows you will actually like your life more and have more peace if you spend more time finding ways to give than trying to figure out how to get more for yourself. This challenges the way we often think about blessings. We tend to think being blessed means a person is getting more.

We all like to receive. Our church buys dozens and dozens of doughnuts every week so we can make them available for free on Sunday mornings in our café. A few weeks ago the doughnut guy stopped by the church office to pick up the check for his monthly invoice. When he came, he brought a couple of dozen doughnuts and gave them to us for free. If a person brings me free dough-nuts, he can count me as a friend for life. I told our financial secre-tary we should never mail the doughnut guy another check. Let's have him always come by the office to pick it up. I'm hoping he'll even bring some doughnut holes next time. It's fun to receive.

Jesus promised that we would be blessed when we give, yet there are few things we worry about as much as money. We stress about how to make more of it, get it to go further, invest it, save it, protect it, and spend it. Do you know how much money you need to feel completely secure? It's the same answer for you as it is for everybody else: a little bit more. Too often we buy into the illusion that what we need to keep us from worrying about money is more money.

When you give away something valuable, it sometimes feels like a loss. After all, you had something and now you don't. That is why Erin's yard sales always make me and our boys nervous. Once she starts wheeling and dealing, we never know what she might sell. I had a Kindle that went missing a while back. She says I lost it, but I'm still convinced she pawned it for five bucks. Either way, for me it was a loss.

Paul saw generosity in a different light. He said it's not a loss. It's an investment in the potential of a future harvest.[2] By sowing your seed, you're creating the possibility for a harvest. He wrote some instructions in that regard to his protégé, Timothy, as he pastored the church at Ephesus: "Command them to do good, to be rich in good deeds, and to be generous and willing to share. In this way they will lay up treasure for themselves as a firm foundation for the coming age, so that they may take hold of the life that is truly life" (1 Tim. 6:18–19 NIV).

> We want to be able to say, "Whether I have a lot of money or only a little, watch how I use money and you'll see Christ."

Once again, Paul connected generosity and good deeds with the same thread. He said doing good and being generous is how we take hold of the life that is truly life. But here's what some of us do. We'll say, "I can't afford to give financially right now, so I'll just be rich in good deeds. I'm not currently able to be generous with my money, so I'll share my time instead." But is that how Paul said we take hold of the life that is truly life? Do we grab it by doing good deeds *or* being willing to share? Does that mind-set reflect trust in God?

Clearly, the answer is no. But we are so good at rationalizing why our situation is the exception. Why? Because we want certainty and want to be sure we can still afford what we want. Our choices reveal that we want a certain lifestyle more than we want the life that is truly life. We trust ourselves to provide what we need more than we trust God.

In fact, do you know what it costs us to not be generous? It costs us being known as loving. One of our goals should be to display Christ through our lives. We want to be able to say, "Whether I have a lot of money or only a little, watch how I use money and you'll see Christ." People should be able to watch how we do our jobs or treat our spouses or handle a stressful situation and make correct assumptions about what Jesus is like. In the same way, we want them to see God's love in us through our approach to handling our finances.

WHAT ARE YOU AFRAID OF?

I went on a mission trip to Ecuador recently. We worked hard all week and it was an amazing experience. The very last day of our trip, we got to be tourists. Our group went to a zip line located in a cloud forest. I had heard of a rain forest, but this was new to me. Evidently a cloud forest is a similar environment to a rain forest in a lot of ways, but the key difference is the altitude. The cloud forest is way up in the mountains, so there is different vegetation and a unique ecosystem.

I've been on zip lines before. Some have been as long as 450 feet and as high as 85 feet. As we prepared to begin the zip tour in Ecuador, we learned that some of the lines were over a quarter mile long. Since we were literally zipping over a valley from one mountain to another, I knew we would be higher above the ground than most roller coasters I've been on. I started to wonder how stringent the building codes were for zip lines in Ecuador. Since I had seen more goats than people in the last hour of our journey to the forest, I realized the line had probably never been inspected anyway. So I had to make a choice. Was I going to have faith in the line and equipment, which would mean I'd either have the ride of my life or die trying? Or would I give in to fear, not take the risk, and ensure that I'd experience neither the thrill nor the pain? I went for it and had a blast.

The root problem that keeps most of us from being more generous isn't greed. It's fear. We want to eliminate uncertainty because it scares us. It is important to realize that uncertainty is a key ingredient to both fear and faith.[3] The difference between fear and faith is how you respond to the uncertainty. When you say yes to giving away a dollar, you are saying no to everything else you could have done with that dollar. If you give in to fear, you'll hold on to it to make sure you can meet your needs. Letting go of it requires a measure of faith.

IN GOD WE TRUST

Jesus knew we'd battle fears over being able to meet our needs, so listen to what He said.

> So do not consume yourselves with questions: What will we eat? What will we drink? What will we wear? Outsiders make themselves frantic over such questions; *they don't realize that* your heavenly Father knows exactly what you need. Seek first

the kingdom of God and His righteousness, and then all these things will be given to you *too*. (Matt. 6:31–33)

He didn't say the stuff we get worked up about isn't important. He said He knows. Then He made us an amazing promise. God promised that when I completely surrender to Him, He will take responsibility for seeing that my needs are met. That is a really good deal. When I put God first and focus on being right with Him, He promises to have my back and make sure I will have whatever I need.

God promises to take full responsibility for a life that is completely surrendered to Him.

At my house, my kids don't worry about food or clothes or bills or anything, except what time they have to go to bed. In the same way, our heavenly Father promises to take care of all of our needs if we will trust Him and put His agenda first.

Jesus asks, "What are you seeking first: My kingdom or yours?" He didn't die on the cross so He could be ranked in the top ten of your life. He won't settle for being in the top three. He is relentless about being number one.

Uncertainty about what could happen tomorrow forces each of us to make a choice about where we're going to put our trust. Most of us live our entire lives trying to steer clear of situations where we'd be forced to depend on God for anything. It's as if we measure success by how little we need God. But if there were never an element of the unknown, we would never need to have faith. God wants us to overcome our fear by surrendering to His purposes completely and knowing He has promised to take care of us when we do. When we consistently ignore opportunities to be generous, I'm not sure how we can think we are following Christ. After all, how can you really say you trust God with your life and your eternity when you don't even trust Him with your stuff?

I'M NOT GREEDY BECAUSE I'M NORMAL

I think most people view greed as one extreme and generosity as another extreme, and they see themselves somewhere in the middle. Certainly there are a few people who are lavishly generous like Mother Teresa. You probably have a picture in your mind of what extreme greed looks like too. You may envision someone such as Gordon Gekko from the movie *Wall Street*. You see yourself somewhere in the middle between those two extremes. Since you personally are not choosing to live in abject poverty and you aren't making multimillion-dollar real estate deals, you consider yourself normal and not greedy.

Perhaps you can even point to how you've made progress in this area and are less greedy than you used to be. You might say, "I used to be constantly pushing to get more and more, but now I'm content." Most of us would probably say that people who aren't trying to earn more and who are satisfied with what they have are spiritually mature and have no problem with greed. But that isn't spiritual maturity.

Greed is not about how much money and stuff you have. It's about how much you are depending on your money and stuff to make you happy. Just because I stop pursuing more stuff doesn't automatically mean I'm pursuing more of God. Just because I have less stuff doesn't make me less greedy. Because having less is not the same as being more generous.

Some of us think there is a magic number and if we could ever accumulate that amount, we would be safe and have no financial concerns. So we start making plans and taking steps to get enough saved to get across that line. I've talked to lots of people who were sure that once they were able to finally cross that line, they would feel secure. Never once have I talked with anyone who was concerned whether that line might also be the point at which they stopped trusting God. But I'm afraid that is exactly what it often is. It's not a conscious decision we ever make, but when our overriding goal is to hit a certain number in our savings account or investments, our trust gradually migrates to our stuff.

We start out saving to be wise, but soon we're saving to insulate ourselves from ever having to trust God.

I've been there. Before I was a preacher boy, I hit a point where my career was on the fast track. We've all heard and likely repeated the old saying: "Money changes people." No one ever says, "Money changes me." But it can. God started blessing me financially, so I decided the best move I could make was to not increase my standard of living. Instead, I began to put every spare dollar into savings. It wasn't so I could be more generous. It was because my trust was beginning to transition from my God to my stash. I think this is where a lot of us struggle. We start out saving to be wise, but soon we're saving to insulate ourselves from ever having to trust God. We forget that God doesn't bless us simply to raise our standard of living, but to raise our standard of giving.[4]

My personal opinion about how you can find the balance between wisely saving for the future and also being generous is to give away at least as much as you save. If we would each do that, we could unleash generosity on our communities at an unprecedented level.

Paul wrote a marvelous letter to the church at Corinth about this very issue. He encouraged them to trust God, rather than give in to fear.

> Now he who supplies seed to the sower and bread for food will also supply and increase your store of seed and will enlarge the harvest of your righteousness. You will be enriched in every way so that you can be generous on every occasion, and through us your generosity will result in thanksgiving to God. (2 Cor. 9:10–11 NIV)

Paul has told us here why God gives us more than we need for just ourselves. It is so we can be generous, just as He is. By leveraging our money and stuff through generosity, we get to demonstrate to the world what a life looks like when God is the star of the show. When we allow generosity to spill out of us, it inspires thanksgiving to God. When someone in our church gives money to provide a backpack of food for a child for the weekend, there is a mom who is thanking God for that person's generosity.

REDEFINING NORMAL

My experience has been that as I grow in my relationship with God, He sometimes stretches me out of my comfort zone. Since the early days of our marriage, Erin and I have always given a tenth of what we received to God by giving it to the church we attended. A number of years ago, God impressed on us that we needed to begin gradually increasing the percentage we gave. We had reached the point where giving a tenth didn't require any faith. It had become routine. So we decided to start giving more. It wasn't an easy shift to make, but we did it.

A couple of years ago, we agreed God was again calling us to dramatically increase the amount we were giving away. We knew that to pull this off we would have to make some significant changes in our lifestyle and indefinitely postpone some purchases we had been hoping to make. I'm not going to lie: it was a tough step to take. Once the decision was made and we were on the other side of it, it was crazy how God began to bless our lives in big and small ways. We never missed the income and enjoyed seeing where it was going and how God was using it.

I don't tell you that story because I'm hoping you'll put me in an elite category of super-spiritual people. The reality is it is absolutely shameful how long it took me to get to this point in my spiritual growth. What is even worse is that my wife led the way and, at times, dragged me along. But I am glad I'm here now because I have learned without a doubt that God's promises are true. Before I got to experience the blessings of a more surrendered life, I had to answer the same two questions you will have to answer. First, do I really believe Jesus when He says it is better to give than to receive? And second, can I set my fears aside and completely trust God with my stuff?

The best way to ensure your hope doesn't migrate to your money and stuff is by deciding in advance how much you are going to give away. I can't stress enough how important it is to settle this decision in advance. Most of us have the same problem with our money as we do with our time: the urgent always seems to crowd out the important. There are bills to pay and the kids need money for their sports league and we have to do as much shopping as possible right away, since everybody knows the Black Friday deals (or whatever sale happens to be going this month) are as good as it gets. Then we take the money we still have left and put it toward savings or paying off our mortgage or starting a college fund or saving for a new truck. The result is we have nothing left to give.

It's not that generosity isn't important to us. We just didn't plan for it. So the importance of being generous gets crowded out by the urgency of paying the bills and saving for the future. Since nobody seems to ever have extra left over that they don't know what to do with, we have to decide in advance where we're going to put our trust.

You might be thinking, *But I have so much debt! If I could just press a magic reset button and at least get back to a zero balance, then I would start being generous.* Unfortunately, that button doesn't exist. God forgives, but your creditors probably won't. So you have to start right where you are. Make the choice to start going in a different direction. I promise you will never regret it.

"WHAT HAPPENED TO MY PIZZA?"

I love pizza. It is easily my favorite food. How can an item that manages to combine cheese, bread, pepperoni, and sausage not be everybody's favorite food? That will always be one of life's great mysteries to me. One time I ordered a pizza and something unusual happened.

The delivery driver rang the doorbell, so I grabbed my wallet and headed to the door. He seemed nervous and fidgety when he handed me the credit card receipt to sign. He kept switching the pizzas from one arm to the other, and I was beginning to worry he might drop them. I decided to help him out and offered to go ahead and take the pizzas and set them down inside the house while I signed the receipt. I'm still not sure what possessed me to do this as I brought them in the house, but for some reason I opened the lids on both boxes to check the pizzas. The first one was fine, but I was stunned to see that the second one was missing three pieces.

I didn't know whether to laugh or cry, but I wanted some answers. I went back to the door and asked the driver why my pizza was missing a few of the slices. He said, "Oh, about that. I got hungry on the way over, and I haven't had time to take a dinner break, so I ate some. Sorry about that."

Okay, it's confession time. None of that actually happened. Can you imagine if it did? That would be wild. It would be like ordering something from Amazon to give to my kids, and the FedEx delivery guy taking it home to his kids because he thought they would like it. We know that isn't how things are supposed to work. Delivery people are supposed to deliver stuff.

Here's the deal: we are God's delivery people. He puts money in our hands, but He doesn't intend for it all to stay there.[5] In that same letter to the church at Corinth, Paul wrote, "At the present time your plenty will supply what they need, so that in turn their plenty will supply what you need" (2 Cor. 8:14 NIV). God gives us more than we need for just ourselves so we can deliver some of it to other people. He recognizes we have wants and needs and doesn't ask us to live as vagabonds. We even get to set our own salary. One of the most important decisions you'll make is deciding what percentage of your income to keep for yourself. He simply asks you to remember it isn't all intended for you.

If you've seen the movie *Cast Away*, then you saw a great example of someone who thought like a delivery person. Tom Hanks played a FedEx employee who ended up stranded on a deserted island. Soon after he was marooned there, some FedEx packages from the wreckage of his plane washed ashore. He opened some of them out of necessity. But there was one package decorated with angel wings that he never opened. When I first saw the movie, I was the obnoxious guy yelling at the screen, "Open it! There might be something awesome in there!" But he thought like a delivery person. He decided he could survive without opening it, so he did. At the end of the movie, he finally made the delivery of that package. If I just ruined the plot for you, I apologize. But you have had a decade to watch it, so I don't feel

> **Here's the deal: we are God's delivery people.**

too bad about spoiling it for you. By the way, the guy in *The Sixth Sense* is already dead. Now I am just being mean, but you should have already seen that one too.

One of the most striking characteristics of the New Testament church was their "no strings attached" generosity. They sold off their possessions so they would have even more money to be generous and meet other people's needs. These were the same disciples who had jockeyed with each other for position by debating who was going to be considered great enough to sit next to Jesus in heaven—yet had been unwilling to wash each other's feet. After Jesus' resurrection, their attitude was radically different, and generosity became a hallmark of their movement. Now they thought like delivery people. It is so exciting to see how today a growing number of churches are moving in that same direction and becoming extravagantly generous.

Perhaps there have been times when you have seen a need and thought, *If God really cares, why doesn't He do something about that? If He really cares about hungry kids . . . If He really cares about the woman who gets beat up by her boyfriend . . . If He really cares about refugees who are forced to flee to another country, then why doesn't He do something about it?* It's a good question. You may not like the answer.

There are certainly some prayers that only God can answer. For example, healing someone physically is something that is completely in God's domain. But for many issues, God's answer to the problem rests with those of us who call ourselves His followers. God wants us to do something about hunger and homelessness and disasters. But for us to respond to those issues, it takes money. When each of us gives some of what God has given us, the result is amazing.

Let me ask you one more question you may find difficult. What would your finances look like if you really believed Jesus is who He says He is and can do what He says He can do? The only way we are going to unleash generosity on our communities is if we decide that God is our Lord instead of our back-up plan.

Can you imagine what will happen in your community if you get this right? You'll start to change the reputation of Christians. You'll be known for how you love others. Your possessions will never possess you. And you will be rich—the kind of rich that really matters. Increase your trust in God and decrease your trust in stuff. It really is the best way to live.

DISCUSSION QUESTIONS

- The man in Luke 6 who interrupted Jesus didn't seem to recognize the greed in his own life. Why does it seem to be relatively easy to see greed in other people and hard to see it in ourselves?

- Even though we don't see ourselves as greedy, there are two ways money can become "giant-sized" in our lives. One way is consuming (we spend it all) and the other is hoarding (we try to save enough to protect ourselves from every conceivable "what-if"). Which flavor of greed is more likely to trip you up?

- What are some of the reasons that keep you from being more generous than you are today? What can you do to overcome these excuses?

- Tell about a time when someone was generous to you with his or her money, time, or influence. How did that person's generosity affect you?

- What does it cost us to not be generous?

- If you believe Jesus is who He says He is and can do what He says he can do, then that truth will shape your financial life. How is that reality going to change the way you handle your money this month?

TELL GOD ABOUT THEM

Outreach has to come from the overflow of a growing relationship with God.

One time when I was almost fifteen, my dad asked me if I was ready to learn how to drive a car. I was super-excited because I equated driving with dating. Since I was one of the oldest kids in my grade, I would be one of the first to be able to drive. This was finally going to be my big break that would give me an edge over all the other guys. I could already envision rolling up to my dream girl's house in our yellow station wagon with wood paneling on the side and a luggage rack on top. We'd have our first date and then would be together forever. It wouldn't matter that I was driving a family sedan. All that would matter was that I was driving.

My dad took me out to a rural, two-lane highway. I was still a few weeks away from being able to officially get my learner's permit, which would mean I could drive as long as there was someone else in the car who had a valid driver's license. I didn't have my permit yet, though. In other words, for the first time in my life my dad was letting me do something illegal. This was shaping up to be a very good day.

As I got behind the wheel, I realized for the first time that our car was a stick shift, rather than an automatic transmission. No big deal. I had been driving cars in video games for years, so this couldn't be too much harder. After all, my parents did it all the time, and like most fifteen-year-olds, I was sure I could do anything better than them.

I'm still not sure how the transmission survived that day. I grinded gears, the car jerked and sputtered, and eventually we got moving. I was cruising along in fifth gear at around fifty-five miles per hour when I noticed blue lights coming from behind me and approaching very fast. I freaked out. "Dad, what do I do?"

My dad calmly said, "Pull over."

Now, I think it's important that I point out what my dad did *not* say. He didn't say, "Slow down, and *then* pull over." So at fifty-five miles per hour, I pulled onto the gravel shoulder and hit the brakes. Gravel started flying everywhere, the car began to skid sideways, and I was sure that whenever the car finally stopped sliding, I would be headed to jail. I just prayed that my dream girl would come and visit me, even though we never

One of the crucial first steps in evangelism that often gets missed is prayer.

got to go on our first date. To my amazement, though, the police officer flew right on past us and continued down the highway. My dad decided the lesson was over and he was going to drive us home.

I had missed a crucial step: I didn't gear down and slow down before I pulled over. Sometimes in life we can inadvertently skip a foundational step too. When we do, sometimes it just gets us off track temporarily and we're able to recover and learn from our mistake. There are other times when we just keep struggling and never realize we have overlooked something basic that could make things easier and better. We just assume it was supposed to be this hard.

One of the crucial first steps in evangelism that often gets missed is prayer. Even though it is one of the last things we're covering in this book, it is where we really need to start our out- reach efforts. Don't start running so fast toward your community that you leave God behind. You aren't going to reach anyone without Him. In fact, you aren't going to reach anyone, period. God does the reaching and saving. He delights in using us in the process, so it's critical that we spend time talking with Him and following His lead.

So often people don't pray because they are convinced it doesn't matter whether they pray. They wonder, *What is the point of asking God for anything if He already knows what we're going to ask? Why should I bother if He already knows what He is going to do?* It is true that God doesn't need us to bring any new information to His attention that He had previously overlooked. He doesn't need for us to make such a convincing argument that we persuade Him to see things differently. So what is the point of prayer?

LET ME INTRODUCE YOU TO SOMEONE I DON'T KNOW

The story of Erin's Strip Church ministry doesn't start with her first visit to the strip club. It starts in an extended time of prayer and fasting she engaged in as she prayed for three very specific things. God answered her prayers during that time in some amazing ways. The biggest answer, though, was something she wasn't praying about at all. While we saw God bring about some definite changes in the areas Erin was praying about, He also brought about a change in her. He gave her a burden to reach out to others, and especially those working at the strip club. That thought hadn't previously even been on her radar.

I have heard lots of people question why they should spend any time in prayer. I've even wrestled with that question before myself. But I have never heard anyone say they wondered if there was any point of talking with his wife or kids. I haven't known anyone who was confused about why she should bother communicating with her friends, either. We instinctively recognize that for those relationships to be healthy, there has to be ongoing conversation.

God is not simply a means to an end for us to solve our personal problems. He is the source of a relationship. I think the biggest reason most people don't pray more is because they view God as a force, rather than a Father.

My phone is equipped with a GPS that talks. Since it talks, I gave it a name: Ethel. When I ask Ethel a question about how to get somewhere, she tells me the answer. She is always right. When I am driving, she is always right there with me. But do I have a relationship with Ethel? No! She's not a person.

It seems a lot of people relate to God the same way they interact with the GPS app on their phones. They know they can ask Him questions and get good answers. They recognize He is always with them. But they don't view Him as a person they can have a relationship with. Outreach has to come from the overflow of a growing relationship with God.

> Outreach isn't a matter of marketing a self-help program. It is an introduction to a person.

There is a series of videos on the Internet called *Comedians in Cars Getting Coffee*. In each episode, Jerry Seinfeld drives a different classic car and takes another comedian to get coffee and share stories. In the season one finale, he goes out with Michael Richards, who famously played Kramer on their mega-hit sitcom.

At one point in the drive, Michael asks Jerry to turn down a certain street and stop in front of a specific house. Michael explains that he knows Sugar Ray Leonard and wants to introduce Jerry to him. In fact, he knows him so well that he thinks Sugar Ray might invite them in.

It turned out it wasn't Sugar Ray's house. In fact, Michael didn't even know him and actually has no idea where he lives. His performance was convincing right up to the point where he was forced to confess. Jerry cracked up.

A lot of people try to do outreach the same way. We hardly ever talk with God in prayer, so the result is that we know about Him but don't really know Him. Then we try to introduce others to the God we're pretending to know very well. That never works.

If Christianity were simply a self-help program, we could recommend it to other people as something that could benefit them even if we didn't have any firsthand experience. But outreach isn't a matter of marketing a self-help program. It is an introduction to a person. We can't introduce others to someone we don't really know.

RESETTING OUR PRIORITIES

As we get to know God in prayer, a by-product of knowing Him is that we get to know His will. As we talk with God, we always discover His heart is for people. Paul wrote to his apprentice, Timothy, about how to pray:

> So, first and foremost, I urge *God's people to pray*. They should make their requests, petitions, and thanksgivings on behalf of all humanity. *Teach them* to pray for kings (or anyone in high places *for that matter*) so that we can lead quiet, peaceful lives—reverent, godly, *and holy*—all of which is good and acceptable before the eyes of God our Savior who desires for everyone to be saved and know the truth. (1 Tim. 2:1–4)

If you ever sense that your desire to reach people with God's love is diminishing, then you simply need to spend some time in prayer. God desires for people to experience the relationship with Him that you have. He wants to reach your community even more than you do. When you spend time in His presence and begin to see the world through His eyes, you'll have a fresh experience of His unconditional love and of the eternal change He can make in lives.

Have you ever tried to watch part of a 3-D movie without wearing the 3-D glasses? The very thing you're supposed to be focused on becomes blurry and out of focus. That's what life is like when we try to live it without communicating with God. Our focus drifts back to ourselves and skews our perspective so that we can quickly lose sight of our mission. We begin to increasingly focus on our own priorities, while the people around us recede into the background of our priorities as they become blurry and out of focus. By staying in communication with God through prayer, we keep His priorities in front of us, and His priorities are that we love Him and love the people around us.

In my community, I did a study on our population and overall church attendance. I learned that if you were to pick ten of my neighbors at random, only two of them will be at any Christian church this Sunday. My best guess is that 80 percent of my neighbors don't have a meaningful relationship with Christ. According to Paul, how many of them does He want to save? All of them. If your community is anything like mine, then you won't have to look far to find someone in need of God's love and grace.

WAS BLIND, BUT NOW I SEE

James wrote about prayer too. He reminded us about the prophet Elijah: "*Remember* Elijah? He was a man, no different from us. He prayed with great intensity asking God to withhold the rain; *God answered his prayers and* did not allow a single drop of rain to fall for three and a half years. It did not rain until Elijah prayed again *for God to open the skies,* when the rain came down and the earth produced a great crop" (James 5:17–18).

As soon as the first notes are played, almost everyone instantly recognizes the song "Amazing Grace," even though it was written more than two hundred years ago. It was originally published by John Newton in 1779, just three years after the Continental Congress signed the U.S. Declaration of Independence. In a letter Newton had written twenty-five years earlier, in 1752, he used the words that would ultimately become the closing line of that famous first verse, "I was blind, but now I see."[1] Even though it isn't a song about prayer, it always reminds me of the importance of praying, especially that last line.

For the sake of full disclosure, I need to tell you I haven't always been a person devoted to prayer. That all changed when our third son, Levi, was born. His birth coincided with the very first meetings we had with some friends about the possibility of launching a new church called Friendship Community Church. Since this was our third child, Erin and I both had a "been there, done that" attitude. We knew life would be different with three children, but since we had already done this twice, we figured this new chapter in our lives would be mostly just more of the same. We had no idea what we were in for.

Levi was only about two months old when we first began to notice he didn't seem to be responding to visual stimulation. He would smile when he heard our voices, but didn't seem to ever make good eye contact with us. In fact, the one thing consistent about his vision was that he *would not* look at us. I would position myself in front of his gaze to try to convince myself he could see me, but he would always look away. In retrospect, I think he must have been looking away from the dark shadow of me and toward whatever light he could see. Sometimes his eyes would shake left and right very rapidly. We needed some answers.

We talked with our pediatrician about our concerns with the hopes that she would tell us we were blowing things out of proportion and should stop worrying so much. Instead, she told us we needed to take our child to a specialist.

The specialist told us Levi had a condition called *ocular albinism.* Just as albinos have a lack of pigmentation in their skin and hair, those with ocular albinism have a lack of pigment in their eyes. Evidently, albinos generally have this vision problem too.

Levi wasn't albino, but his lack of ocular pigment meant the macula of each eye was underdeveloped. One of his symptoms was *nystagmus,* meaning his

If God can give physical sight to someone experts said was beyond hope, then with God there is no one beyond hope.

189

eyes would shake back and forth when he tried hard to focus. We asked what we needed to do to get Levi's vision corrected. The specialist said there was no treatment or surgery for this condition. He was legally blind and it was not correctable, and glasses would do nothing to improve his sight.

"What does that mean? Will he have a normal life? Will he go to a normal school? Will he ever be able to see a football when I throw it to him?" The specialist said there was a 66 percent chance he would need to attend the blind school, and there was 0 percent chance he would ever drive a car. Erin cried. I was just numb.

> Before Levi came along, when I prayed, I would always give God an "out" when I asked Him to do something.

I grew up attending a small, traditional Baptist church. I could count on one hand the times I'd seen anyone anointed with oil as James 5:14 describes. But I was desperate, and I knew God was the only one who could do anything about it. So we called everyone we knew and asked them to come to a special time of prayer where we would anoint Levi's head with oil and pray for our son to be healed. Lots of people came, and it was a moving experience as we prayed together for a miracle, and then everyone went home.

Before Levi came along, when I prayed I would always give God an "out" when I asked Him to do something. I would make my request, and then I would say something like, "But Your will be done." There is certainly nothing wrong with praying for God's will to be done. We should always want God's will to be done.

But when I prayed, I didn't say it because I was seeking God's will. I said it because I didn't think God was really going to do anything in response to my prayer anyway. I said it to let Him off the hook. I said it because I didn't have any faith. But not this time.

I prayed boldly and unashamedly that God would heal Levi's eyes. I began to notice for the first time that when people prayed in the Bible, their prayers were even bolder than mine. They didn't cushion their prayers with loopholes and escape clauses. Over and over, I read how people had brazenly asked God to do what they knew only He could, and often God answered their prayers in amazing ways. James wrote that sometimes God responds to "prayers offered in faith" (James 5:15). As I continued to pray, my faith grew even though there was no obvious change in Levi's condition. The more I prayed and asked God to heal his vision, the more I became convinced that God *was* going to heal his vision. It wasn't because I thought I was anything special. I am a nobody from nowhere. But I kept reminding myself that Elijah was a man just like me. I had access to the same God, with the same power as him. So that meant anything was possible.

After a few months, some of my friends asked me, "Hey man—how much longer do you want us to keep praying about this? When are you going to just accept it?" I told them they could probably go ahead and stop praying, because they didn't have faith. For them to keep praying would be a waste of their time. But I was never going to stop praying until Levi could see. Elijah had prayed seven different times that God would make it rain, until He finally did. Elijah didn't interpret God's initial delay as a denial. He had persisted and kept praying, so I was determined to do the same thing.

God has miraculously answered our prayers. Each year when we take Levi back for his annual checkup with the specialist, he looks into his eyes and says there is even more pigment now than there was the previous year. The uncorrectable condition continues to be corrected. It is hilarious to sit in the room and listen to Erin and the specialist talk past each other. The specialist will talk about how these things sometimes just happen and there is no explanation. Erin always clarifies that it didn't just happen; there is an explanation, and His name is Jesus. They each just keep repeating their points as if they haven't even heard each other. I don't care whether the specialist gives God the credit, but I will never talk about Levi's eyes without fully acknowledging how He answered our prayer.

Levi's vision is now better than mine. He wears glasses (as do our other boys), but only to correct the astigmatism that he inherited from me. I don't know what I'll be able to do when my other boys turn sixteen, but I decided when he was only six months old that when Levi is sixteen, I am buying him a car. Then he is going to drive me to the annual checkup with the specialist. And I am going to say to the specialist, "Na-na na-na boo-boo. You said this could never happen." Of course, I will do it all with love in my heart and in Jesus' name.

Here is what God has taught me through all of this, besides the fact that I shouldn't taunt the pediatric low vision specialist. If He can give physical sight to someone experts said was beyond hope, then with God there is no one beyond hope. There is nobody you will ever lay eyes on who God doesn't love. There is nobody you will ever meet who God can't reach and give them eyes that see Him clearly.

Jesus taught us, "Keep on asking, and you will receive. Keep on seeking, and you will find. Keep on knocking, and the door will be opened for you. All who keep asking will receive, all who keep seeking will find, and doors will open to those who keep knocking" (Luke 11:9–10).

Perhaps you know someone you have started to wonder if God could ever reach. Maybe you have a family member or friend you have been praying would move toward God for a long time, and you're just about ready to give up. You need to know He can reach even the person you think is the most unlikely candidate to ever change or want anything to do with God. So don't stop praying. Keep on asking in faith. Elijah was a regular person just like you. You have access to the same God with the same power. He can do it. He may even answer your prayer by using your act of kindness as the catalyst that encourages the person you love to take the next step toward Christ.

PRAY BEFORE, DURING, AND AFTER

As I have started running again, I have been reminded of the importance of drinking water before, during, and after a big run. It's crucial to stay hydrated. When a runner gets even 2 percent dehydrated on a warm day, it begins to affect his performance.[2] That is why smart runners keep water with them at all times.

Pray before you serve. Just as water is essential to running, prayer is essential to outreach. We saturate our servant evangelism projects with prayer before, during, and after. We're relying on God to grow the seeds of kindness that we sow.

At our daily staff meetings and our monthly churchwide prayer experience, we pray in advance for our servant evangelism projects. We pray that our volunteers will have fun, will begin new relationships, will step out of their comfort zones, and will effectively demonstrate God's love to everyone they come in contact with. We also pray that God will orchestrate divine appointments. We recognize that we are completely dependent on Him to connect us with people who are ready to take the next step toward Him as they experience an act of Christian love. On the day of the project, we give instructions to the teams and then have one more brief time of prayer as we begin to serve.

Perhaps you're planning to do your project on your own and don't know of anyone interested in helping you share God's love with your community. Pray about that. Jesus said, "The harvest is plentiful but the workers are few. Ask the Lord of the harvest to send more workers into His harvest field" (Matt. 9:37–38). Ask God to connect you with others who are ready to plant seeds and ultimately be part of the harvest.

Pray as you serve. When people receive an unexpected act of kindness, it is astonishing how open they often become to prayer. When you ask folks if there is anything specific you can be praying with them about, some will still say, "No, everything is good right now." Their prevailing assumption is that if they don't have any problems, then they don't have anything to pray about. But many will share with you about what they are dealing with in a very candid and sincere way. When that happens, be ready to say a very brief prayer for them. This is not the time to show how impressively you can pray by talking like someone in a Shakespeare play. That would probably freak them out. Simply ask God to let them see Him in their situation, and pray that they will continue to experience His love in the days ahead. That's it.

We also encourage people to keep us posted on anything specific we pray with them about. We want them to recognize when God is working in their lives. When we pray about something knowing there is no way it will happen unless God intervenes, then it focuses us so we can't possibly miss it when He moves in the situation. So we give them basic informa-tion about our church so they can follow up with us later and tell us what happened in the situation we prayed about. While we want them to be able to connect with us by attending our weekend worship experience if they are ready to take that step, we are far more interested in them remembering God's love than remembering us. We want to make God famous.

Don't stop praying. Keep on asking in faith.

When I buy someone's lunch at Subway, I sometimes tell them that I had prayed that God would choose just the right person to be in line behind me, and God chose them. People are always grateful to know that I had prayed for them before we even met, and they are touched by the thought that God had orchestrated this act of kindness just for them.

Pray after you serve. As we conclude each servant evangelism project, we gather all of our volunteers together to share stories about our experience. We have a brief prayer for everyone we were able to touch and for any specific prayer requests that people shared with us. Jesus did something very similar when he reconnected with the seventy people he had sent out on a mission in teams of two. They excitedly reported on their experiences, and Jesus prayed with the group (Luke 10:17–24). We encourage our volunteers to continue to pray that God will keep working in the hearts and lives of the people we met long after the project has ended.

FASTING FOR A CHANGE

Whenever Erin shares the story of Strip Church, one of the topics she is asked about most often is the fast she was doing when she was first moved to begin reaching out to the employees of strip clubs. For some of us, fasting is as unthinkable as shaving our heads or walking across a fire pit. If it hasn't been part of your experience yet, it may seem like a strange ritual. What image comes to your mind when you picture a person who fasts? A health nut? A guy who hears voices in his head? A cult leader in a robe?

When we think of fasting, we should probably think about Jesus. Not only did He practice it, but He expected that we would too. Check out what He said:

> And **when you fast,** do not look miserable as *the actors and hypocrites do when they are fasting—they walk around town putting on airs about their suffering and weakness, complaining about how hungry they are. So everyone will know they are*

fasting, they don't wash or anoint themselves with oil, *pink their cheeks, or wear comfortable shoes. Those who show off their piety,* they have already received their reward. **When you fast,** wash your face and beautify yourself with oil, so no one who looks at you will know about your discipline. Only your Father, who is unseen, will see your fast. And your Father, who sees in secret, will reward you. (Matt. 6:16–18, bold emphasis added)

I think the reason the spiritual discipline of fasting is so misunderstood today is because of a widespread lack of awareness. Most regular church attenders have probably never heard a sermon on the topic. Yet it is mentioned in the Bible more times than something as important as baptism. So it is a topic we really can't afford to overlook.

In this passage from Matthew, Jesus gave us a negative command, a positive command, and a promise. First, when fasting, don't neglect your appearance for show. If you walk around looking like a bushman who badly needs deodorant, then you have the wrong motive. Second, rather than looking like a starving scavenger, do it for an audience of One. God knows about your fast and is the only one who needs to know. Third, He promises that you'll be rewarded. Each time God asks for a sacrifice, He promises a blessing.

My first experience with fasting was when I took an elementary nutrition class in college. I needed an elective, so I thought, *How hard could a nutrition class for future elementary education teachers be?* As a bonus, I figured I would be one of the only males in the class, which could only help my chances of making a love connection. What I didn't know was that the course was taught by a five-foot tyrant of nutrition, and this was the one class that every education student at my school dreaded.

Our assignment was to record everything we ate or drank for six weeks. We also had to accurately calculate the number of proteins, fat grams, vitamins, lipids, and lots of other things I had never heard of. By the end of the second week, I was on a bread-and-water diet just so I didn't have to do all those calculations on everything I ate. I wasn't fasting for any spiritual purpose. I was fasting because I was lazy. I ended up dropping the class and picked up bowling as my elective. It was taught by one of the football coaches, so everything worked out great.

I have found that fasting does not change the way God hears, but it does change the way I pray.

Fasting as it was taught and practiced by Jesus is not a diet or something to do just so you can check it off your list. It is denying your appetite for a spiritual purpose, so you increase your appetite for God. In our consumer-based culture, we're not big fans of denying our cravings. We have ravenous appetites for thrills, experiences, and certainly food. While food-related fasts are not the only type, that is what fasting is normally about.

At my house, there are some days when we decide our kids have watched enough television for the time being. So we tell them they need to say no to television for a while, so they can say yes to reading a book or playing outside. As parents, we recognize the importance of our kids getting exercise and stimulating their imaginations and creativity. While they generally comply, they don't always agree that we have the right idea. But as parents, we have a different perspective. If we have bigger and better perspectives than our kids, just imagine how much bigger and better God's perspective is than ours. Jesus taught that it is important to sometimes say no to food for a while so we can say yes to an increased appetite for God.

The starting point to fasting is a hunger for God's viewpoint and power. Spiritual hunger leads to fasting, and fasting leads to increased spiritual hunger. Fasting is not about me trying to get God to hear my prayers differently and perhaps reconsider His options. It is not going on a hunger strike to force God to tap out and submit to my demands. It is about me opening myself up to move toward what He wants. I have found that fasting does not change the way God hears, but it does change the way I pray.

If you have never practiced fasting before, I would encourage you to do it as you prepare to reach out to your community. There is no command about how often or how long to fast. God gives us this discipline as an opportunity, so we can use it to seek Him more as often as we desire. So whether you eat only fruit or abstain from carbs or don't eat anything at all, you get to decide how you will fast and how long you will fast. Be careful not to get caught up in someone else's rules or in thinking there is only one right way to fast. Make a plan, and then spend some extra time in prayer. I think you will be surprised by how your perspective changes, especially in regards to reaching your community.

STAY CLOSE AND YOU'LL GO FAR

The truck I drive is getting near the end of its life cycle. I plan to drive it until it dies. It seems as though every week a different light appears on my dashboard. So I have developed a system. If the warning light isn't red, I ignore it. Since I don't want to invest any more money into my truck than absolutely necessary, I figure yellow and orange gauges aren't severe enough for me to worry about. But red gauges get my attention. Those are the ones that keep me from running out of fuel or overheating the engine or anything that would cause my truck to break down.

The people who finish well in life aren't necessarily the smartest or richest or most talented. The ones who finish well are those who pay attention to the right gauges. Your personal time with God is the single best thing you can do to stay focused on the most important gauges in life. Praying, fasting, and spending time in the Bible will keep you close to God so you can increasingly see yourself and your world with His perspective.

You are the only person with your background and specific life experiences. You are the only person with your personality and sphere of influence. God has a plan to use you to make a difference. When I read the Bible, I don't find many stories about megachurch movements. But I find story after story of God using individual people who are completely surrendered to change their community. I am praying for you as you take your next steps and start a movement in your community that will have repercussions for eternity.

DISCUSSION
QUESTIONS

- What do you struggle with the most when it comes to praying and communicating with God?

- One big reason we never get around to praying is because our relationships (even with God) usually don't seem urgent. What steps can you take to ensure that your conversation with God continues to be both important *and* urgent?

- One reason persistence is so important in prayer is that it focuses us. When we're dialed in on a specific prayer request, there's no way we can miss when God answers it. Tell about a time when God clearly answered your prayer.

- In today's culture there seems to be a lot of talk about the power of positive thinking. Sometimes people even think it's the same thing as prayer. What are some of the differences between prayer and positive thinking?

- If parents of small children have a bigger and better perspective about what's best, just think about how much bigger and better God's perspective is than ours. How does it make you feel to know that sometimes you might not understand why God is answering your prayer the way He is?

- Fasting is when we replace the time we would have spent eating with time spent talking with God through prayer and reading the Bible. People have fasted throughout history when they faced major decisions, to find clarity and direction. Even

Jesus fasted. Have you ever fasted? How did that go for you? What did God show you through that process?

- As we get focused on saying yes to God, rather than trying to get Him to say yes to us, we'll begin to discover His agenda. First Timothy 2:1–4 reveals that His heart is always for people. What specific person or what group of people is God burdening you to reach with His love? What are you going to do about it?

WRITE THE NEXT CHAPTER

Servant evangelism is not a program. It is a way of life.

Our oldest child, Elijah, introduced our family to *Doctor Who*. If you have never heard of it, then you are in the same boat I was in six months ago. It is a serial science fiction television show that has been broadcast on BBC for more than fifty years. The Doctor is a time-traveling humanoid alien who solves crises and saves the world on a weekly basis. In case you were wondering, it is not based on a true story.

In a recent episode, we met a civilization known as the Ood. They were introduced as a species that was created entirely to serve. In fact, the Doctor was told that if they didn't serve, they would shrivel up and die. Because he is so brilliant, though, the Doctor knows there must be more to the story. He reasons that no species would ever naturally evolve into being servants, so he senses that something is amiss. Of course, he discovers that an evil mastermind has enslaved the Oods for his own nefarious purposes, and the Doctor is able to set them free and save the day.

I found it fascinating that the Doctor's initial assumption was that no species would naturally evolve into being servants. It seems that our culture has the same assumption. Yet that is exactly what Jesus expects His followers to increasingly become. In a culture where everyone is focused on his or her own agenda, serving others stands out as unusual. When the serving is rooted in Christ's supernatural love, people recognize that what they are experiencing defies a logical explanation. They are drawn toward God through our selfless and sacrificial acts of kindness.

So how do you reach a stripper? The same way you reach a banker, a computer programmer, a cosmetologist, a mechanic, a real estate agent, a contractor, a stay-at-home mom, and an unemployed dad. You love them the way Jesus loved you. You demonstrate your love for them through meeting needs and generously doing acts of kindness, regardless of how they may have treated you in the past. You pray for them and invite them to take the next step toward Jesus from where they are. And you watch God grow the seeds that you plant.

Servant evangelism is not a program. It is a way of life. As you become the person God intends for you to become, you never know who He might use you to reach.

KATIE'S NEXT CHAPTER

When Erin first met Katie in the strip club, neither of them had any idea where the road ahead would take them. Katie's faith has grown tremendously. She amazes me with her insight and maturity as she continues to trust God one step at a time. She writes in her prayer journal every day and loves diving into the Bible. A few weeks ago, I found out that she has made it her habit to pay for the person behind her each time she goes through a drive-thru. She does this to show God's love to others, even though as a single parent she isn't always sure how she is going to make ends meet for the month. But God always provides for her at just the right time. She sees His hand explicitly in blessing her with a job, a home, a vehicle, furniture, clothes, food, and Christmas gifts for her kids.

Just this week she was contacted by the metro police chief and invited to take the civil service exam. If she passes that, she will then go to the police academy and be on her way to realizing her dream of being a police officer. She got the call from the police chief on the last day of a three-week fast that she had undertaken to know God more deeply. She is one month away from completing her associate's degree in criminal justice. She has straight A's and perfect attendance.

Katie now joins Erin on her visits to the strip club as they take meals and gifts to the dancers, bouncers, and managers, and then talk and pray with them. Last Sunday (while she was still in her fast that

As you become the person God intends for you to become, you never know who He might use you to reach.

we didn't find out about until later), a new dancer from the strip club showed up at church for the very first time. Katie had been inviting this girl to church for a while. On Tuesday, we found out that this girl had taken her own step of faith and quit her job at the club. So the cycle is repeating itself as another girl takes her next step toward Christ. The step of faith that Erin took, and then Katie took, paved the way for hers.

Katie has become the person we've described in this book that we all need to become. She is known for how she loves others. She meets people where they are and invites them to take the next step toward Jesus. She extravagantly meets needs and does acts of kindness, even toward those who may have used her in the past for their own purposes. She is generous and prays and fasts for God's perspective. She is not a stripper. She is a beautiful child of an amazing God who loves her very much, and she wants everyone else to experience the same life-changing relationship with Him that she has. I am so proud of her.

YOUR NEXT CHAPTER

When our kids were toddlers and we were teaching them to walk, we would always get their attention. We got in front of them so they would try to come to where we were. We would sometimes even hold up a reward, like a Cheerio, to motivate them to want to come to us. Sometimes they would stumble and fall. When that happened, we never said, "I guess you just weren't cut out to be a walker. I don't ever want to see you fall again, so let's stop doing this." Our kids never thought, *I'd rather settle for crawling for the rest of my life than put myself through that again.* We knew they could do it, so we kept encouraging them and helping them as they grew stronger and better at it.

As you begin to take your first steps in servant evangelism and reach out to your community, there will probably be times when you stumble and fall. Everything is not always going to go perfectly. Don't lose sight of the fact that Jesus has gone in front of you and is calling you to follow Him. Just as He did when he called Peter to take a step of faith out of the boat, He will give you the power to do it. He never calls you to sink.

Sometimes we sink when we take our eyes off of Him, but that is never His intention. He wants us to focus on Him and keep moving forward. The more we train our minds to focus on Jesus, the less we will be discouraged and the stronger our faith will grow.

So take the next step forward and watch what God does in you and through you. If you choose to trust God completely and follow Him without holding anything back, the worst thing that can happen is you'll get to experience exactly what God wanted you

The worst thing that can happen is you'll get to experience exactly what God wanted you to experience.

to experience. If that's the worst that can happen, then you don't have a lot to lose.

If you want more resources or want to continue the conversation, then come visit us at BeKnownForLove.org. You get to write the next chapter of the story. I know it is going to be a good one. I can't wait to hear about it.

NOTES

CHAPTER 1

1. Larry Osborne, "Where to from Here?" (sermon, North Coast Church, Vista, CA, May 6, 2007).
2. See Steve Sjogren, *Conspiracy of Kindness* (Ventura, CA: Regal Books, 2003), 135.
3. See Tim Stevens, *Vision: Lost and Found* (Centreville, VA: Exponential Resources, 2012), 125.
4. Rhonda J. Sholar, "Big Challenge, Great Idea," *Outreach* magazine, January–February 2014, 81.

CHAPTER 2

1. Andy Stanley, "Our House" (sermon, North Point Community Church, Alpharetta, GA, January 15, 2006).
2. See Dino Rizzo, *Servolution* (Grand Rapids: Zondervan, 2009), 178–179.
3. Dorothy Day, *The Duty of Delight: The Diaries of Dorothy Day* (Milwaukee: Marquette University Press, 2008), September 17, 1961 entry.

CHAPTER 3

1. Originally published by Engel in *Church Growth Bulletin* in 1973, his idea was later republished in James F. Engel and Wilbert Norton's *What's Gone Wrong with the Harvest* (Grand Rapids: Zondervan, 1975); see page 45 and the footnote.

CHAPTER 4

1. John M. Darley and C. Daniel Batson, "From Jerusalem to Jericho: A study of situational and dispositional variables in helping behavior," *Journal of Personality and Social Psychology* 27, no. 1 (1973): 100–108.

CHAPTER 5

1. Simon Burnton, "50 stunning Olympic moments No28: Dick Fosbury introduces 'the flop,'" *Guardian* (UK), May 8, 2012.
2. Jim Burgen, "See No Evil" (sermon, Flatirons Community Church, Lafayette, CO, August 24, 2008).
3. State Fair of Texas, Food Finder, accessed January 22, 2014, http://www.bigtex.com/sft/nav/foodinformation.asp.

CHAPTER 6

1. See John S. Dickerson, "How Christians Should Respond to Hate," *USA Today*, September 21, 2013.
2. Carey Nieuwhof, "How to Reach Unchurched People Who Don't Think They Need God," May 10, 2013, http://careynieuwhof.com/2013/05/how-to-reach-unchurched-people-who-dont-think-they-need-god/.

3. See Sadhana Kapur, *Great Women of India, Mother Teresa* (New Delhi: Learners Press, 1998), 17–18.
4. Ian Walton, "Small Things: Mother Theresa [sic] and Mandela's Rugby Jersey," *1Africa*, July 19, 2013, http://www.1africa.tv/small-things/#.Upd1OSjkHG0.
5. David Scott, *A Revolution of Love: The Meaning of Mother Teresa* (Chicago: Loyola Press, 2005), 121.

CHAPTER 7

1. See Andy Stanley, *Fields of Gold* (Carol Stream, IL: Tyndale House, 2004), 52.
2. Ibid., 51.
3. Ibid., 16.
4. Randy Alcorn, *The Treasure Principle* (Sisters, OR: Multnomah, 2001), 75.
5. Ibid., 76.

CHAPTER 8

1. Jonathan Aitken, *John Newton: From Disgrace to Amazing Grace* (Wheaton, IL: Crossway, 2007), 228.
2. Karen Asp, "Sipping Points," *Runner's World*, June 1, 2010. Accessed March 12, 2014. http://www.runnersworld.com/drinks-hydration/sipping-points.

ABOUT THE AUTHORS

Todd Stevens is the pastor of Friendship Community Church, one of the fastest growing churches in America. Friendship is known for finding creative ways to show God's love in the community, and over 90 percent of the regular attenders are involved in service opportunities. Todd is also a church consultant in the area of servant evangelism. For more information about his ministry, visit FriendshipCommunityChurch.org or BeKnownForLove.org. You can also follow him at facebook.com/todd.stevens or twitter.com/PastorToad.

Erin Stevens is the founder of Nashville Strip Church, a ministry that reaches out to the employees of strip clubs. She and her husband Todd met while they were each pursuing their MBA. She enjoys spending time with her family, public speaking, homeschooling her three boys, and practicing her mad scarf-making skills. For more information about her ministry, visit NashvilleStripChurch.com. You can also follow her at facebook.com/erin.stevens.

REFRACTION

GOD ALIGNS PEOPLE OF FAITH TO HIS PURPOSES

Thomas Nelson's Refraction collection of books offer biblical responses to the biggest issues of our time, topics that have been tabooed or ignored in the past. The books will give readers insights into these issues and what God says about them, and how to respond to others whose beliefs differ from ours in a transparent and respectful way. Refraction books cross theological boundaries in an open and honest way, through succinct and candid writing for a contemporary, millenial-minded reader.

COMING SOON

OCTOBER 2014   APRIL 2015

Watch for more at RefractionBooks.com